BACKROADS BOSS Lady

Happiness Ain't a Side Hustle—Straight Talk on Creating the Life You Deserve

JESSI ROBERTS

FOUNDER OF *Cheekys*

WITH **BRET WITTER**

GRAND CENTRAL PUBLISHING

NEW YORK   BOSTON

Grand Central Publishing
Hachette Book Group
1290 Avenue of the Americas, New York, NY 10104
grandcentralpublishing.com
twitter.com/grandcentralpub

First Edition: March 2019

Grand Central Publishing is a division of Hachette Book Group, Inc. The Grand Central Publishing name and logo is a trademark of Hachette Book Group, Inc.

The publisher is not responsible for websites (or their content) that are not owned by the publisher.

The Hachette Speakers Bureau provides a wide range of authors for speaking events. To find out more, go to www.hachettespeakersbureau.com or call (866) 376-6591.

Interior spot art used with permission from Cheekys

Library of Congress Cataloging-in-Publication Data

Names: Roberts, Jessi, author. | Witter, Bret, author.
Title: Backroads boss lady / Jessi Roberts, Founder of Cheekys and Bret Witter.
Description: First Edition. | New York : Grand Central Publishing, [2019]
Identifiers: LCCN 2018037099| ISBN 9781538745731 (hardcover) | ISBN 9781549113468 (audio download) | ISBN 9781538745717 (ebook)
Subjects: LCSH: Businesswomen—Idaho—Biography. | New business enterprises—Idaho. | Success in business—Idaho. | Cheekys (Firm)—History.
Classification: LCC HD6054.2.U62 R63 2019 | DDC 338.7/687092 [B] —dc23
LC record available at https://lccn.loc.gov/2018037099

ISBNs: 978-1-5387-4573-1 (hardcover), 978-1-5387-4571-7 (ebook)

Printed in the United States of America

LSC-C

10 9 8 7 6 5 4 3 2 1

CONTENTS

POSTED BY ME IN AN ONLINE BOUTIQUE-OWNER FORUM AUGUST 11, 2017

Looking for some support ~ I am really needing a place to reach out and am hoping this is it!!

For those of y'all who don't know me I am Jessi and am the founder of Cheekys aka The Bosslady ~ and wow things have gotten crazy around here...I kinda feel like when I was young and had too much to drink and needed to put one foot on the floor! 😂

This last year we had HUGE growth. I started this baby in 2011 and that was only because I knew I wanted to do something in my tiny town and I didn't want it to be a laundry mat. And in Jan of this year we did as much business as the entire year of 2014. Each month we have increased at least 20 to 100% in growth. We have had to get new machines for printing (which led me to realize how expensive power is and how much weight an old building can hold), we have overloaded the PO [post office] in our town and have no idea

what to do there, we have hired 30 plus people to help us...
and the list goes on and on.

So in 2016 we were featured by *Inc.* magazine and then
shortly after I was contacted by several publishers about
having a book. That contract is now signed and my writer
(who is helping me a ton) shows up tonight to stay for a
month. Let me tell ya writing a book is NOT at all how I
thought it was. We are getting contacted constantly about TV
shows, reality TV, movies and all kinds of stuff. They just can't
believe that we have this business in such a small town and
that it's grown the way that it has.

I still love all the designing aspects; the manufacturing
is my all-time favorite. I LOVE to help other women and am
working on a consulting/mentoring program now with a
few gals. And it's what I really want to do. I am hoping my
book will do that for women on a budget, women who just
have questions and hope it moves them. I have let a handful
of women in this group read the first book proposal and it
seems to be headed down the right path.

Okay, all that being said...I am in a bit of a whirlwind. I
still am so involved in everything down to the tissue paper we
use. I am kinda overwhelmed by all this attention. I prefer to
be behind the scenes...I love typing but not being live or on
TV. It's scary to be so vulnerable and exposed. Living up to the
perception people have is hard. I am not fashionably dressed,
I don't do a lot of makeup, I am in a bun most days...I am
overweight. I don't have loans or a line of credit, I cry like

once a week (half good tears, half the time sad)...this voting finals thing [for boutique of the year] has me thrown for a loop. I am sooo proud of all the girls on there and sooo many of them carry our line which makes me even more proud. So I guess my question is: how do we stay sane, stay private, how do we give our opinions without sounding like a bully or arrogant? These are the thoughts I have everyday...please tell me I am not alone.

SS: First of all can I say that you hardly wearing makeup, having your hair in a bun, and being overweight is 100% relatable and what all of us women REALLY want to see...

KWB: I want to hug you...

GB: I am proud of what you have accomplished and especially from a small town...

VCW: Omgah Jessica Dawn Roberts...such a freaking amazing and inspirational story. YOU are who so many of us strive to be...

LM: I don't have any advice really but I just want you to know how happy I am to have found Cheekys...

VS: You are so not alone!!

You know what, girls? It's been more than a year since I wrote that post, and I'm still terrified to put myself out in the world. There are things in this book I really don't want to talk about and things I am terrified for you to know. But it's support like this that makes me feel like I can—and that sharing my life and advice can do some good in the world. So to everyone who bought from Cheekys, wrote to Cheekys, and posted on Facebook asking for support. To all the boutique owners and the moms-in-business and the small town girls working for it every day...thank you. I love you. This book is for you.

IS THIS A BUSINESS BOOK?

That's the first question my publisher asked, after they said they wanted to work with me (celebration time!): "Is this a business book?"

Understand, I hadn't written it yet. They had read a twenty-page proposal that grew out of a small article about me in *Inc.* magazine titled "How This Former Outback Steakhouse Waitress Built a $2.8 Million Retail Brand." So obviously, business was important.

But is this a business book? No. Not really.

Don't get me wrong. If you are looking for business tips, you will find them here, especially if you own, manage, or work at a small business. After all, I went from a tiny store in an even tinier town to owning and running a multi-million-dollar national brand. So I have tips, and lots of them. I have "life experience," as they say. Everything I know about selling I learned in the car business. Everything I know about running a boutique I learned by trial and (so, so many) errors. I've had to learn how to find products for nothing and make an extra twenty dollars a day to put food on the table for my kids. I've also had to learn how to design and manufacture on an international scale, wholesale to three thousand boutiques, and manage thirty employees. In other words, I've learned a lot.

But this isn't one of those "ten things that will make your business explode" books. I don't have a set of principles to unlock the secret of success, right now, in all your life's ventures. I don't want to shift paradigms or scramble business logic. I've never been invited to a TED Talk. They don't want someone like me. I never went to business school. In fact, I dropped out of Robert E. Lee High School in Midland, Texas, two months before graduating. My business advice works, because it's had to work. I didn't have the luxury of failure.

But there is so much more to my story. I'm a working mom from a lower blue-collar background (and that's putting it mildly). I live in a horseshoe-shaped town in Idaho. I'm from the country, I sell clothing and accessories to women in the country, and I love being from, in, and for the country. Thanks to some book called *Hillbilly Elegy*, there's a perception in cities like New York (where my editor lives) that people in small towns should be pitied, because we're too stupid and lazy to know our lives would be better in the city. Well, I don't believe that at all. I've lived in Texas. I've lived in Boise. I live in New Plymouth, Idaho, population 1,538, because I want to live here. I want to raise my kids here. And I run a company for all the women in all the little towns like New Plymouth who feel the same way.

This book isn't for the CEOs, the Wall Streeters, or the TED Talkers. It's for the mom-and-pops fighting for the money to open tomorrow. The business owners working fifteen hours a day, six days a week, to put food on the table. The wives running companies out of their bedrooms to keep their families afloat. The moms working double shifts and selling cosmetics on the side. The factory workers. The mail carriers. The people living on the backroads, and I don't just mean in rural areas, I mean any place that is overlooked and discounted, where the hustle is harder and each dollar means more. Most of us don't get $10,000, and definitely not $100,000, to get started on our dreams. Most of us don't even get emotional support. So this book is for you: the strivers, the hustlers, the never-give-uppers who never had savings, investors, or outside help, because that's my story, too.

This book is for the moms working sixty hours a week selling cars or slinging trays so their children can have a better life. I've been there. I know how it is. I know it can feel like people look down on you, no matter how successful you are. I will never look down on you, girl. You're my hero.

Being a Boss Lady isn't about money, after all. It's not about glamour—thank God, because I am the opposite of glamorous—or a big idea that changes the world. I didn't start an Internet company. I didn't even start a website, although I have a very successful one now. I founded a retail store, in a small brick building with a big plate-glass window, across the street from the Double Diamond Saloon. That seemed like such a bad idea even the local bank wouldn't give me a loan. They said, "You can't open a shop in New Plymouth, Jessi. There's so little traffic we drive lawnmowers down the main street."

"Sure," I said, "but only during the co-op races, and that's two days a year."

They still said no.

I built Cheekys anyway, and to this day, despite more than $20 million in sales, I have never been approved for a bank loan for my business. I have never been offered money by an outside investor, although my best friend (we were single moms together) has been a silent partner since day one. I still run the business out of New Plymouth, even though it has exploded worldwide. In 2012, Cheekys' total revenue was $43,000. *For the year.* That's gross, not net. Six years later, our revenue is $125,000 *every week.* Our sales are increasing by more than $100,000 a month. By next year, at our current growth rate, we'll hit a million dollars a month in sales.

Now let me be clear: that doesn't make me rich. I still don't have money in my bank account or the backyard pool I've been dreaming of since I was a little girl. Okay, I have a pool, but it's the collapsible aboveground kind from Bi-Mart, which my husband says is barely better than the way we did it when we were kids: rainwater in a stock tank. (I don't wanna spend this whole book explaining terms, so if you're in the city and don't know what a stock tank is, get your Google on.) My husband and I, who both work at Cheekys full time, make $2,000 a month, and we only started paying ourselves in 2016. At one point, Justin became frustrated by that. Our Yukalade—the half Yukon, half Escalade body-shop special we'd been driving for ten years— had broken down again.

"Jessi," he said, "everyone who works for Cheekys has a new car but us."

"Yup," I said. "And we provided those opportunities, Justin. We helped those families thrive. Doesn't that make you feel good?"

Call me crazy, but I take more joy in knowing Erika can care for her five children, including two she took in after her brother died of cancer way too young, and the other Erica can buy a minivan for her growing family, than I ever would in a swimming pool.

That's why I invest almost everything Cheekys makes back into my business and my community. That hurts me financially, I suppose, but it makes me rich in the things that matter more than money. I give my four children, ages ten to eighteen, a comfortable home with plenty of love and attention. I set a good example of hard work, kindness, and entrepreneurship. I work with my husband every day (in different buildings, to keep the marriage going!). I provide a good living to thirty employees, mostly women, who make me laugh inside our anthill, as we call the warehouse and order center, even when the orders are piling to the ceiling. Soon, if things go as planned, I'll have a new warehouse and an expanded 2,800-square-foot destination store in New Plymouth (twice as many feet as residents!) to provide a retail anchor and community gathering point and, hopefully, bring thousands of visitors to this gorgeous, struggling, frustrating, infuriating, perfect little town.

And I have my Chicks—the thousands of mostly rural and small-town women who are fiercely loyal to the Cheekys brand. I don't advertise much, except on Facebook. I don't pursue publicity. Every order is checked by me and processed by my staff, even though we now have more than 50,000 individual customers and 3,000 stores carrying the Cheekys line. I've grown my business on word of mouth by offering clothing and accessories that small-town women love, but I've succeeded because I offer something they want even more: respect for their lifestyle and a personal connection. Cheekys isn't just a boutique. It's a worldwide community that celebrates small-town life and helps ordinary women see the beauty inside, the opportunities outside, and the value of who they are.

In other words, I set out seven years ago to feed my six-person family, and to help my small rural community, and I ended up building a family bigger than Boise. It has not been easy. It's been a struggle. The journey has been gritty and desperate, and at several points I almost failed. I've had my family shattered and my confidence shaken. I've been attacked so ferociously that I've had to build my love (and I have a lot of love for the people in my life) out of the pieces of my broken heart. I've made a million mistakes. I make mistakes every day. But running Cheekys has been the most rewarding "job" I've ever had. These Chicks are my family, and you know I am proud to be the Head Mother Clucker to this brood of hens (and a few roosters, too). I'm proud of what we've built. But I'm even more proud of the way we did it, with respect for one another, a ton of hard work, and love for every person, even the haters who put us down.

So, no, this isn't a business book. It's a book *about a business*. It's a book about family: the one you have and the one you create. It's a celebration of small-town life, but it's honest about the downsides, too. It isn't a guide. It's a story. My story. The

Cheekys story. I'm writing it because I want you to say to your-self, "If Jessi can do it, I can, too." The word *it* doesn't mean start a small business, although there are plenty of tips for that here. *It* means grabbing hold of your personal dream and living your Boss Lady life.

I want everyone who reads *Backroads Boss Lady* to feel the way I feel every night, when I sit in my U-line camp chairs in the backyard of my farmhouse two miles outside New Plymouth, Idaho. From there, I can look over the alfalfa fields of my neigh-bor, Dave, to the steep yellow cliffs that climb toward the Saw-tooth Mountains. It's a gorgeous sight. I'm from West Texas, a place that pretty much defines the words *flat* and *empty*; I still can't believe I get to look at mountains every day.

But I can also see my little round collapsible swimming pool, and our print shop five feet behind it, and the cargo containers on the edge of our gravel parking pad. I can see the two Trae-gers smoking dinner and the new outbuilding my husband is building—he keeps calling it a "man cave" for some reason, even though it's obviously a "hen den"—and the pile of scrap lumber he left next to the six-foot-tall "chicken mansion" he built for our six layers last year, complete with plastic chandeliers.

The younger kids are swimming or running around. My eighteen-year-old, Hunter, is shambling off with his best friend, Kolby, who's basically been living with us. Friends are over drinking Coors Light with Clamato juice in it, which Justin claims is an old Idaho tradition. The mosquitos are biting, but it doesn't matter, because we're laughing about what happened at work that day, and answering Facebook requests from Cheekys customers, and talking about what we're going to do in the ant-hill tomorrow, because most of the friends who come over at night are the people I work with every day. I'm sure there is a book that tells you not to invite your employees to your home, but I can't imagine living any other way.

This is Boss Lady, y'all—even if the pool is above ground. *This is happiness.* This is what the dream looks like for me and millions of others like me. And it's here for you. It's not impossible. Anyone can achieve it. No matter where you live, where you come from, or what you've been through, you can have your own house and your backyard barbeque and your chicken mansion, by which I mean whatever you call success. It takes hard work. It takes smart work. It takes staying true to your values and never giving in, but this is America: anything is possible.

Especially in Idaho.

CHAPTER 1

WELCOME TO NEW PLYMOUTH

Payette County, Idaho, is an hour northwest of Boise along Interstate 84. For the first twenty minutes of that trip, the drive is through suburban communities, with the steep desert mountains known as the Boise Foothills off to the right. Past Caldwell it becomes rolling farmland—mostly the deep green of sugar beets up against the dry sagebrush of the high plains—and then eventually the scrub prairie of the open range. The Bureau of Land Management (BLM) land is green in the spring but yellow most of the year, and empty except for the occasional herd of cattle local ranchers have paid the government to let them graze. On the left, it's rolling land forever, without even a tree; on the right, the mountains are like cliffs, rising a hundred feet to a flat plateau, with the jagged purple peaks of the northern Rockies in the distance. It's beautiful, but for me the most welcome sight is the small turbine power plant that comes suddenly into view, alone on the range at the top of a long rise, because from there the road dips down into the Payette Valley, the first place in my life I've comfortably called home.

The Payette Valley consists primarily of small farms crosscut with canals leading from our two local rivers, the Payette and the Snake. The valley used to be covered with apple orchards; now it's mostly cattle ranches, dairy cows, and field crops. No potatoes (that's eastern Idaho), but plenty of corn, peppers, pumpkins, and onions, along with alfalfa fields sprouting blue flowers in the fall and bright yellow mustard and canola fields and the sharp green mint that make the valley smell like breath freshener when it's cut. Payette is the biggest town in the area, with 7,500 residents. Fruitland, with a population of 4,500, is the fastest growing. Some old-timers grumble that the Fruit-landers think their shit don't stink because they have most of the new construction, but why pick a fight? I like Fruitland. They're country like the rest of us, and they have my favorite coffee shop. It's a drive-through window connected to a garden center. Half the population in the valley is Mormon, and Mormons avoid caffeine. For the rest of us, coffee is life.

My town, New Plymouth, is the smallest in the area and the farthest from the center of things. It was founded in 1898 as a utopian farming community by businessmen from Chicago who thought irrigation canals were the next world-changing innova-tion. They built their "New Plymouth" (our high school team is the Pilgrims) in the shape of a horseshoe so each homestead could have access to a large field fed by canals. The three-block commercial artery, Plymouth Avenue, cut the short way through the center; the industrial area sat between the horseshoe's open ends. Little two- and three-bedroom houses soon filled in the rest. Even back then, New Plymouth was famous for the wooden waterwheels that lifted water out of the irrigation canals.

One hundred twenty years later, New Plymouth is that rarity of modern life: a town that's basically the same as it was in 1900, even if only three of the original twenty-two waterwheels remain. Back when Plymouth Avenue was part of the fastest route between Portland and Boise, the downtown was full of shops, but after they built the freeway six miles away in 1957, New Plymouth slowly returned to its origins as an isolated farming community. There's a small open-sided lumber mill that halves standard-cut boards with hand-fed band saws; on the other edge of town, there's a small fertilizer depot for local farmers. Otherwise, it's two bars, a bank, a gas station, two restaurants (the burger place has been for sale for three years), a farm co-op, and a liquor store inside a three-aisle market. One block of our historic one- and two-story downtown was leveled to build the tan stucco headquarters of our largest local company, a web portal called Truckstop.com. The rest looks almost exactly like it did in the photographs of New Plymouth from the 1920s. The town has almost as many churches—fourteen—as businesses.

I didn't move here for the businesses or the churches. I like to joke that I came here to retire. (Ha!) My husband, Justin, and I met in Boise, but we lived in Texas for our first two years together. I grew up there, in Wichita Falls. I was used to the hard, flat emptiness of the west Texas desert, where it's a hundred miles to the next town with nothing much to see in between. Justin hated it. He grew up on his dad's ranch outside Homedale, Idaho. He liked the high prairie. He liked being rooted. He liked Clamato juice in his Coors Light. It was too hot in Texas for a guy raised with snow tires on his pickup truck.

So we moved back. After a year of being unsettled—staying with friends, working on a car lot to make ends meet, you know the drill—we leased our dream home. It was next to a dairy farm about a mile outside a little no-stoplight town I'd never heard of called New Plymouth. The dairy meant poop, which meant flies, especially when the wind wasn't blowing, but the house had four bedrooms, a long driveway, and plenty of land.

In Texas, I worked full-time. I had been working full-time to support myself, in fact, since running away from home at fifteen. I eventually dropped out of high school, rented an apartment with no furniture, and slept on the floor. I had no friends in Texas. No family relationships I hadn't burned to the ground. I was an outcast kid, the kind local people had pointed at with suspicion since I was six years old, no matter what I did or how hard I tried, and I was tired of it. I saved enough money for a bus ticket. I went to the library and found the town with the youngest and most educated population in America. I wanted to party with those kind of people.

I got off the bus two days later in Provo, Utah.

Provo's a Mormon town. They don't have liquor stores. They don't have bars. They don't even drink caffeine. I couldn't believe it. I said, "What do y'all mean, y'all don't drink Dr Pepper? Everybody drinks Dr Pepper."

Within a year, I was back in Midland, Texas, working forty

hours a week at a jewelry store in the mall, and I'd worked full-time ever since, even as I became a mother four times over between the ages of twenty and twenty-eight. I was working right up to the day Justin and I left Texas, when my youngest was two months old. I was managing a used car lot in Odessa for the man who gave me my big break in the car business after I left my first husband at twenty-two. (He cheated while I was pregnant. We'll get to that.)

Justin is a worker, like me. He had been spraying pickup bed liners as a side job since he was twenty-one. In Texas, he was Mr. Mom to our four children, three still in diapers, while resealing industrial storage tanks in his spare time. We decided that in Idaho, with a partner, he could turn his sealing experience into a business. That's how I "retired" to the easy (yeah, right) job of being a full-time mother to four children and Justin's office manager, taking calls and handling the business accounts out of our house.

I couldn't believe it. I got to be mom! So many women complain about watching the kids, but for me, it was a dream. I'm not a Mormon, but I know their faith well, and I love their emphasis on family. Every night, they have something called the Family Meal, where everybody sits down over food and talks. I never had that as a child. My mother never cooked me a sit-down meal. But ever since Provo, I had wanted that kind of family.

It took me fourteen years, but finally, here I was! A house. A husband. The time and space to be a mom. My oldest, Hunter, was in middle school and obsessed with video games, but Jack,

Sterling, Addy, and I lived all four seasons outside: long walks in the summer, climbing hay bale mountains in the fall, snowball fights all winter. That spring, I planted my dream garden, almost an acre of beans, tomatoes, corn, and every other vegetable you'd ever want. The kids took their tiny "tools" and gardened with me every day. Pretty soon, we had a few pigs we were always chasing down the ditch, a few LaMancha mini-goats the children absolutely loved, and a bull named Zeus.

We didn't have much money, but it was more fun to make everything anyway. Justin and Jack built robots out of boxes, because even at four, that kid loved to build. When Sterling wanted a clown car he could ride in for Christmas, Justin stripped down a Little Tyke cop car and decorated it with colorful vinyl seats, a clown painting, an umbrella, and a honking horn. I stitched Hulk costumes out of green fabric and Justin painted on the muscles. Our kids lived in costumes. Sterling loved Spider-Man so much we called him Peter Parker for a year. Addy always dressed up like Sleeping Beauty. At Ponderosa State Park, Justin and Hunter, our Boy Scout, set up the tent, built the campfire, and caught fish for dinner. The park had trees to the sky, a massive lake, and a paved area where the younger kids could speed around on their training-wheeled bikes with their superhero capes flying out behind them. I mean, how perfect is that? I was an American housewife—the kind who cooked what she raised and canned so many vegetables her husband had to build her a bigger pantry. For a year, our family bowed our heads over my home-cooked meals and finished

every prayer with one of the little ones piping in, "And thank
you to Zeus."

Zeus was delicious, too.

We're country. That's how we roll.

I thought we'd roll like that for years, maybe the rest of our
lives. But it didn't happen. Justin's business failed.

When it started in 2007, the economy was booming. Work
was plentiful, so Justin quickly hired four crews and financed
specialized equipment and trucks. But profit margins were
always slim. We bid so low on some projects, we barely made
money. Even during the good times, the company was scraping
by. That's fine. Most small businesses operate day-to-day. But
when the housing market crashed and took the economy with it,
contractors started squeezing. We had to cut our prices or they
were going to cut us.

Now there was no profit, so Justin and I doubled, then tri-
pled our efforts to find more work. We took jobs in Montana,
Nevada, and even Utah. Justin had a specialty license in bombproof coating (yes, it's real, and it's cool as hell). That brought in
business, but he was the only certified bombproof technician in
the company. That meant he had to be on every job site. By 2009,
Justin was traveling 320 days a year for physically demanding
work, much of it performed inside huge, corroded metal tanks
buried underground. He had severe pain in his neck and back.
He was sick with a cough and...severe digestive problems, let's
call it that. He was pushing his body to breaking, and we were
still falling behind.

Then Justin's partner quit. He was a great guy, an old friend of Justin's whom we loved, but he didn't care about coatings. He had been a mechanic for thirty years; he just wanted to try something different. And he didn't have an entrepreneur's drive. Justin and I were killing ourselves to make the business work, but his partner was pulling away. He couldn't deal with the fact that, because there was often nothing left after the employees got paid, we weren't getting regular paychecks. After all, for thirty years, he'd been paid every two weeks.

So he declared bankruptcy. It wasn't just the business that was the problem. This was 2010. He was underwater on his mortgage, his 401K was in the crapper... Everyone was going bankrupt. He held the loans on the company's trucks, though, so one day, without warning, they were repossessed. Now nobody could get to a job site. Just like that, in one second, a business that had been struggling along for two years collapsed.

And my family's life was destroyed.

We were saved by a client in Utah. When the company went under, they bought our repossessed coating equipment from the bank and hired Justin to train their people to use it. It was a smart business move, because they had a lot of tanks to repair, but it was also a favor. They loved Justin, and they wanted to give him work.

That's the thing about Justin: everybody likes him. Everybody. He's calm. He's funny. And he's helpful. Always. If you don't like me, fine, I understand. If you don't like Justin, you stink. I'm not saying he's perfect, but he's a good man. I've been with bad men, so I know. Maybe that's why I married him.

No, I married Justin Roberts because he's fine looking *and* he's a nice guy. I don't care if you've gained thirty pounds (of red beer) since our wedding, Justin, you're still a sexy man to me. I love your Dad-bod.

The people in Utah loved Justin, too. They loved him so much, they asked me, "How much money would it take for you to be happy with Justin working down here for us?"

They were basically offering him a position at a salary of his choice, but I was honest with them. "It's not about the money," I said. "I just want my husband home and healthy."

They gave Justin a three-month contract on generous terms. Then they gave us a free car—a ten-year-old half-Yukon (the front), half-Escalade (the back) that we dubbed the "Yukalade." Justin and I had driven the 800 miles to Salt Lake City in a single-cab pickup, because it was the only vehicle we owned. The Rock Candy Mountain Resort owners (great people, great name!) were not about to let us drive home the way we'd come down, with our six-member family crammed in the cab.

What they really did, though, was give us a chance to breathe. They allowed us the space to think about the future. I didn't want to go back to selling cars. I didn't want Justin to go back on the road. Like a lot of women, I didn't start my business to get rich or change the world. I started it to put food on the table and keep my family whole.

I often hear other business-owning gals say: "Well, I'm stuck here because of my husband's job." Or "I can't move and this town is too small." That's an excuse. That's another way of saying: *It's not my fault I'm failing.*

I have some advice on that: Stop wishing, and start looking at what you've got.

After all, a business consultant would tell you to never, ever, ever open a shop in a place like New Plymouth, Idaho. The population is too small; the downtown is more than half empty; it's not on the road to anywhere, not even Emmett (population 6,700), twenty miles away. New Plymouth is what some call a destination location. You don't show up here unless it's your destination. So there's no traffic. No out-of-town visitors. The average house in New Plymouth sells for $25,000, and the average resident is retirement age, so there's not much disposable income, either.

Well, guess what? None of that mattered to me. New Plymouth was my home. I wanted to live here.

And in the end, that's the right location: where you want to be.

So I flipped the question. Instead of asking: What location will work for my business idea? I asked: What business idea will work for my location?

What did New Plymouth, Idaho, need?

There was an obvious answer: a Laundromat.

I thought about it, Justin and I discussed it, but I didn't want to spend my life handling my neighbors' dirty underwear. One washer and dryer in my life is enough, thank you. That's another rule to remember: if you don't enjoy the work, don't own the business. Just get a job. It's a hell of a lot easier.

I had noticed something about New Plymouth, though: outside of the churches and maybe the liquor store, the town offered nothing for women, young or old. There were no clothing shops, no gift shops, no yummy soaps or smells when you walked in any doors, no bakeries, no sit-down sandwich shops to chat in, or hair salons, or nail salons, or places to buy much of anything other than a beer, a spark plug, or an overhead door.

That was the opportunity. A women's store would not only help my family, it would help the women in my community. In downtown New Plymouth, rent was only $400 a month for a 900-square-foot space. That was less than $15 a day. If I could make $200 in sales a day, I figured, I could run a viable business.

Surely I could make more than that, right? After all, I knew how to sell. I'd trained in the car business, and I was good. People say it all the time: Jessi could sell ice to an Eskimo.

I find that statement extremely misleading. First, it's Inuits. That's what they call themselves. "Eskimo" is an insult that means "raw flesh eaters."

Second, I would never sell ice to Inuits. Inuits don't need ice. I would never sell someone something they didn't need. That's a slimy salesman, not a good one.

I would sell hand warmers to Inuits, though, which sounds easy, until you think: How would you source the right warmers? How would you transport them to the Arctic? Would the Inuits trust you? Would they even open their doors? Would they care about your fancy product? After all, they already have gloves.

So you know what I would do? I would get to know the local glove maker, so I'd understand the needs of the community, and I'd sell the hand warmers to him. I might even source new gloves for him, ones with a pocket to hold my products. Then I'd set up a relationship with the Inuits to sell their ice to someone else. After all, that ice wasn't just a condition to live with; it was an opportunity. There's always someone, somewhere—like in Hawaii or the Sahara desert—who needs ice.

Success isn't about the killer idea. After all, I wasn't the first to see the need in New Plymouth. There had been places for women over the years: a tanning salon, a clothing store, an antiques shop. They had all gone out of business.

Success is about incremental change: evolving an old concept into a slightly better idea, then putting in the effort to make it work. I didn't want to offer the women of New Plymouth one thing, like my predecessors. I wanted to offer everything: tanning, nails, hair, merchandise. I wanted my store to be a meeting spot where women could tan together, pretty up, buy gifts or matching jewelry over conversation. I knew I couldn't compete on price with the Walmart in Ontario, Oregon, twenty minutes away, and I couldn't compete on inventory with the Internet or the big chains in Boise. I needed to sell an experience: a fun, easy, inexpensive afternoon that was both a shopping trip and a getaway. Oh, I built up quite the fairy tale. I was really stretching that dollar in my mind.

"I'm going to call it Tangibles," I said. Justin was on top of a ladder, hanging the curtains I had cut and stitched by hand for our living room, and he kind of turned away so I couldn't see his face.

"Are you sure, Jessi?" he said.

"It's a great name, babe. We'll offer tanning, and we'll have gifts, which are tangible, because you can touch them and buy them. See what I did there. Tan…gibles. Get it?"

Justin groaned. "Yeah, I get it, Jess. I just don't like it. Do you have any other ideas?"

"I don't need any other ideas. 'Tangibles' is perfect."

I heard snickering behind me. "Um, mom..."

"I know what I'm doing, Justin," I said, a little too proud of myself.

"Well, I think you might wanna come up with other ideas," Justin said, stretching for the last hook. "That's all."

"Um...mom."

"No, Justin. I'm not coming up with new ideas. Tangibles works."

"Mom..."

"Tangibles is..."

"Mom!"

"What?" I said, turning on Hunter, who had been trying to get my attention. "What is it, son?"

"I don't think you wanna go with Tangibles, mom. It sounds like Tan Your Balls."

Justin busted out laughing. Leave it to my smart-aleck middle schooler to explain why everyone was going to fall off their ladders laughing at my store.

"I just want a name that's fun," I said, slumping onto the couch. I'd been trying to come up with a name for weeks, and it was killing me. "I want something sassy and fun and female and cheeky and me. Why is that so hard?"

"Why don't you name it that?" Justin said.

"Name it what?"

"Cheeky."

And that's what I did. I named my company Cheekys—with that all-important "s" to distinguish us from competitors—because of a word I happened to throw out in frustration in the middle of a conversation with my husband and son. But you know what? That's how life works. You can plan all you want, but you won't brainstorm your way to success. The graduate student who designed the Nike Swoosh was paid thirty-five dollars, because the company owner, Phil Knight, didn't like it. Steve Jobs named his company Apple after a trip to an orchard because he thought the name sounded fun. (Must have been a nice farm, because are apples really that fun?) Those things didn't start out with value. They weren't genius ideas. They just held a place until hard work made them mean something.

And besides, Tangibles would have been a terrible name. You know why? Because my idea for a tanning salon in New Plymouth totally and completely failed.

CHAPTER 2

A GIRL'S GOT TO FLEX

A lot of boutique owners are overwhelmed. They post on the Hub, one of our online girl hang and support groups: "You megas [the industry term for large boutiques like Cheekys] have it easy. You have employees. You have thousands of customers. You have a show booth and a store. I'm struggling. I'm working out of my garage. I'm hungry. How can I ever get where you are?"

My answer? Same as a few pages ago: Start with what you got. What's working *for you*? What's not working *for you*? What little thing—ten customers, ten good items, ten dollars—can you build from?

Don't worry about what everyone else has. Embrace *the next step*. And realize this: We've all been there. We all started with no trailer, no booth, no store, no market, no customers, no business contacts, and no followers. So if you want to follow my path, don't look where I am, look where I was.

I started Cheekys with $7,000. I know that seems like a lot. I know many of you have more like $700, but that was everything Justin and I had. Every penny. And it was going out the door every day: for food, clothes, gas, car payments, and the lease on our house.

I wanted a nice store. I wanted a country feel, with raw wood and shiplap siding, like Chip and Joanna do it on *Fixer Upper.* (Love y'all!) Stores were paying $10,000 or more trying to look like an old barn, but good news: we lived on a farm. So Justin pulled down one of the three dilapidated barns out back of our house. He used the worn-out planks and corrugated metal siding to cover our walls. He built displays out of old, knotty throw-away lumber. I bought tables at yard sales and refinished them myself, so instead of looking cheap they looked cool. We painted the store barn red and peach (nekked-body peach not amazing yummy peach), not because I liked those colors together—I hated them together—but because the last tenant at our house had left a bucket of barn red and a few cans of peach paint in the storage shed. Even after I bought two tanning beds on Craigslist, we came in a few hundred dollars under budget, so with the last of my money I bought a half dozen handbags, a dozen pieces of jewelry, and a pile of hair bows and tutus to display in the window looking out on Plymouth Avenue. Yeah, the store was pretty empty, but I learned real fast how to display for effect.

I know what many of you are thinking: I don't have a Justin. I hear it every day on the Hub: "My husband thinks my business is dumb. My husband makes fun of me. My husband thinks I'm dumb. He won't help with anything. He's says I'll never make it. He says I should quit. *I feel so alone.*"

I know I had it good, girls. I know, in a lot of ways, I had it easier than most. I've studied the boutique industry. Fifty percent of owners start out rich. They didn't earn it, so they'll never understand. Of the rest of us, about 75 percent have either no spouse or no support from their spouse.

If that's you, girl, do not give up. *Find somebody.* Your mother. Your sister. The friend you've been scared to open up to about your dreams. Even another shop owner might help, because a lot of us understand that we're sisters. We're in this together. I'm not talking about money. No one is gonna give you money until you earn it. I'm talking about someone who will listen when you bitch, who will give you good advice, and who can run your business in an emergency.

That's why, even though I had Justin, I made my best friend, Trisha, a partner in Cheekys from the start. When I met Trisha in 2003, we were both single mothers with young sons. We hit it off because we loved business—she ran a local trade show company and I was selling cars—and we starting hanging out at each other's houses almost every night. Trisha was a caregiver by nature, and she took care of me. That was the year I started an advertising company, lost it after being injured in a serious car accident, then got knocked up…with twins.

Trisha stepped in. She cooked for me. She did laundry for me. My son Hunter was six, and Trisha wasn't just his babysitter, she was his second mom. She was someone I admired and trusted, because she kept her life balanced between work and the people she loved. When I was with her, I felt safe, like someone was looking out for me, no matter what. You know what I mean? Trisha was the big sister I never had.

I couldn't talk to Justin about Cheekys. I mean, we talked, but he just told me I was wrong about everything. It's hard, because even when they're supportive, husbands have trouble surrendering control. And emotional support? Talking about fears and feelings? No, no, no. I needed Trisha for that. For two years, Trisha didn't do anything for Cheekys but listen to me bitch. She didn't even offer advice. She just said, "What do you think is right, Jessi? What's in your heart? If you believe in it, go for it. It will work." I needed that so much, you don't even know.

Or maybe you do. Because we all need a Trisha, right?

But if you don't have a Trisha, don't worry. You're strong. You can make it. And you will find your Trisha eventually—in an employee, a new friend, even a customer, because I've had so many customers over the years who have become employees and friends. Keep an eye out for the person who makes you feel supported and empowered, because even the best husbands, girls, have trouble with that.

That's not to say Justin wasn't my partner, too. Cheekys was a true family business. We were open from nine a.m. to eight p.m. six days a week, with Sundays off. The store, by necessity, became the center of our family life. We didn't go on many camping trips anymore. We didn't make elaborate costumes (the boys were too old now anyway). In the spring, I didn't plant a garden—haven't had one since, and I miss it every April. Hunter went to school two blocks away. He checked in at the store every afternoon, but spent most of his time with his friends. Sterling and Jack, who were in first grade, went to school a half hour away in Payette. Justin picked them up every day and brought them to the store. He did every errand, from grocery shopping to merchandise pickup at the post office. He didn't like being behind the counter. On Wednesdays, I volunteered as room mother at the twins' school, leaving Justin alone in the store for six hours. That was pretty much his definition of torture.

It wasn't a picnic for me, either, because Justin sucked at selling pink sparkle tees.

It's hard! Running a store isn't just standing around hoping customers buy. People who work regular jobs in retail don't understand that. They get a paycheck, no matter what happens, so they don't push themselves. That's why, when they start their own stores, they often fail, because they don't have the desperation. They don't sell like their kid's next meal depends on it.

In the car business, if you don't sell, you don't get paid. That doesn't mean you pressure people; it means you pay attention to every customer. What do they want? Why did they come here, instead of somewhere else? What is their goal on this visit? How do I get them to walk off this lot not just with a new car, but the *right* new car, the one they'll love, at a price that's fair to both of us?

My grandpa, Daddy Joe, had a brutal but true saying: "You can shear a sheep every year, but you can only cut its throat once."

In other words: Don't sell them merchandise; sell them on the store so you get their future business, too. That's why high-pressure sales don't work long term. If you figure out what motivates a person, and you make the deal fair…you win. You sell them today and the next time, too.

Of course, that takes focused time with a customer, which isn't easy with a four-year-old crawling on your back. We couldn't afford a babysitter, so I raised my youngest, Addy, in the store. She had a play area in the back room with a little wooden stove, washer, and dryer that Justin built, and she loved it. She was in her own world, happily ignoring me…until a customer came in. Then she was pulling my shirt or jumping into my arms while I wasn't looking or standing on my feet saying "mommy, mommy, mommy, mommy, mommy, mommy, mommy," while I tried to point out a lovely new purse. It was so nice when Sterling and Jack showed up after school. The kids loved entertaining one another.

In the evenings, Justin and I took turns in the store so one of us would always be at Jack and Sterling's T-ball games, Hunter's school band concerts, and Addy's 4-H club. More often than not, it was Justin on parent duty, lucky man. He attended every meeting, bought every raffle ticket, made more ground beef tacos than any man I have ever met, and brought dinner and the kids to me every night when I was working late. It wasn't like Chip and JoJo's big reveals, when the kids show up with fresh-baked muffins, all hugs and kisses. It was more like, "Don't run, stop yelling, do your homework, and don't kill each other, mommy's got a customer."

Many women wear shirts that say they want a love like Chip and Jo's. I don't, because I love the love I have. I love my crazy kids. But I would also love one of those muffin days…

Successful selling, though, is more than just being there eleven hours a day. And it's more than attentiveness. Retail success means knowing your market. What is the easiest thing to sell? *Something the customer really wants.*

I thought I knew my market in New Plymouth, but boy, I was wrong. I envisioned a bunch of happy moms and daughters having a weekly bonding session, but hardly anyone tanned. Most of those who did use my most expensive investment (half my start-up budget) were young girls who probably shouldn't have been baking their skin.

I had made a classic blunder: I'm a pasty white girl, and I wanted to tan. But I didn't need to sell what I wanted; I needed to sell what New Plymouth wanted.

That's fine. Nobody gets it right every time. Steve Jobs famously failed three times, and he changed the world. Leonardo da Vinci thought he could fly by turning a screw. Seriously. So everybody screws up (ha ha!), even da Vinci.

Unlike those geniuses, though, I didn't have a margin of error. I had to make money, fast. Fortunately, I already had the solution. No one wanted to tan, but those purses and accessories I put in the front window? They sold out in a week.

I took half the money I made on those sales and bought food for my family. The rest I invested in more merchandise. Clearly, there was a market in New Plymouth for what would eventually define Cheekys: cute clothes and accessories you could actually afford and still enjoy wearing, whether working your day job, heading to 4H with the kids, or dancing with cowboys at the Double Diamond Saloon. I had no interest in $200 purses or designer pants. We're working-class and proud of it in New Plymouth. I wanted merchandise that cost less than thirty dollars—under twenty bucks was the goal—but was well made, stylish, and worked for a country girl. Southwest Idaho is ranch country. I wasn't selling clothes to bust broncs or farm in, but I sold inside that style set, because I liked that style, and that's what my market wanted.

In short, I let my customers shape my inventory...within reason. As a storeowner, you have control of your inventory. Open the door, and sales reps come flooding in with catalogues, offering discounts. I fell for it. Everybody does. Justin convinced me, for instance, to buy hundreds of dollars' worth of Boise State merchandise...just before I realized almost everyone in New Plymouth loved their main rival, the University of Idaho Vandals. I still haven't been able to get rid of those orange-and-blue cell phone holders. Anybody looking for a deal?

Still, even at the beginning, I had a good idea what I wanted Cheekys to stand for. That's why I never took consignment. It's tempting, because consignment fills your store at what seems no cost, but there is a cost: you lose control of your inventory. You are no longer curating your store or brand, and I insisted on controlling every aspect of my brand. (That's why I shoved that Boise State gear in a box and hid it in the garage. It could affect my other sales.) If someone asked me about consignment and I liked what they had, I bit down hard and bought it from them, even if it cost me every dollar I had.

But I never settled. I made sure each item in Cheekys was exactly right. If a local craftsman came in, I said, "I like that shelf, but can you make it in robin's-egg blue? Can you add my knobs to your dresser? I think my customers will like that better." I worked closely with a local carpenter who built birdhouses out of fence posts. I told him I'd buy three if he changed the colors. Then I asked him to build me some tables and chairs in the same style. Everything sold, I reordered, and both of us were happy. I have one of his tables in my living room today.

Then I started buying fabric from mill-end factories and scrounging coupons for the Joann's in Ontario, Oregon. I found grandmothers at local craft fairs who sewed and paid them by the piece to make American Girl doll clothes out of my fabrics. Doll clothes were a hot market, but the selection from suppliers was weak. I had a feeling customers were buying what was available, not what they liked. So I made American Girl clothes in the Cheekys style, and my sales spiked. Soon, those craft-fair grandmas were sewing aprons and other higher priced items out of my discount fabrics.

You have to be flexible, even when you're firm. You have to adapt to what your customers are buying, because their taste will differ from yours. It's putting together all the opinions—yours, theirs, even Justin's. That's how I developed my doll clothes. Addy never liked dolls, but I looked at my sales numbers, and it was clear a lot of other little girls did. Today, I encourage my staff to check the sales numbers as much as possible. All revenue streams are updated daily on a whiteboard in my office. I break down best-selling items weekly. I want my employees to study what is doing well. Not just what is selling, but where—online or in the store? Which categories are growing? Which are declining? Is it poor inventory choices, or is our customer base shifting? Are we making poor design choices? How do we respond?

Nothing is too small to matter. When I worked at a Subaru Mitsubishi dealership, I studied where the easiest and highest profit customers parked. Sounds crazy, but it worked. The most impulsive customers always parked in the same two spots; the hardest customers with the lowest sell-through always parked on the opposite side. Whenever someone pulled into the second and third parking spot on the right next to the service department, I was out the door to greet them. I left the difficult costumers to others. Just that one change, and my sales spiked four cars a month—that's about $25,000 a year in commissions.

I recently looked at the sales numbers from my first year in business, and I was surprised to see how many children's items Cheekys sold. I sell so few children's items anymore. But early on, my customers were from New Plymouth, and the town had an older population. These were rural women; they didn't spend money on themselves. But they loved buying for their grandkids.

So I stocked wooden toys, butterfly wands, and hair bows, along with the jewelry, clothing, and purses that make up the heart of my business. My best-seller was tutus for little girls. They came in different colors, so I made a giant wall display and sold them for five dollars each, the perfect price for impromptu granddaughter gifts—and a very inexpensive way to make the store seem full. Even now, local women sometimes ask why I don't carry the tutus anymore.

My most important sale that first six months, though, was

the tanning beds. As soon as I realized tanning wasn't working, they had to go. Never bang your head against a wall! Take the door instead.

I ended up selling the beds for more than I bought them for, and in all honesty, that was probably the only way Cheekys stayed in business the first year. Justin had to deliver them to the buyers, and they weighed a ton. (Not literally, but almost.) One buyer was a rich couple, probably from California, who lived in a mansion in the mountains a few hours away. Justin and his friend had to carry the bed up the curving stairs and down a long hall to the "sitting room" attached to the bedroom. They almost crashed it into the huge cage blocking half the hall.

"Oh, that's for the monkey," the man said.

"Ahhhh...did you say monkey?"

The dining room had a huge table with only two chairs and an infant's high chair. "That's for the monkey, too," the man said. "He usually eats with my wife."

To this day, Justin thinks we should get a monkey. "He could sit right there," he says, pointing at the side table next to his lounger. "We could eat Slim Jims together." My Lord, that man loves small creatures.

He also loves carpentry and plumbing, thank God, because once the beds were gone Justin transformed the area into a salon for two hair stylists and a nail technician. I laugh, because every chapter in this book could be called "Justin builds something new for Jessi." He complains, of course, but he'd be lost without his tools. Justin is the kind of guy who, if he doesn't have a project for five minutes, he's out tinkering under his lawnmower or hauling a pile of lumber to a friend's house or "putting in the ground work while he can," aka digging pipe trenches for a job he may get to at some point down the road. He has a contractor's license, and he can do just about everything. I call him my "98 percenter," because Justin is fantastic at knocking out the first 98 percent of a job. But hanging that last bathroom door? The ceiling fan? That section of baseboard he didn't have enough lumber to finish? He tends to be on to another job before he gets around to those.

Fortunately the salon he built was beautiful, and it proved more successful than tanning. Women don't need tans, after all, but they do need their hair done. *Why hadn't I thought of that?*

Within weeks, I had a steady if small income from renting my two hair stalls and a new group of customers to up-sell on purses and bracelets. The nail salon didn't go as smoothly. The first girl I hired didn't know how to do nails. Then a local woman asked me to build a special booth for her. I gave up my office for that rental, but a few days before she was supposed to start, we discovered she didn't have a nail license. She told everyone she decided to work out of her house, and since I didn't have anyone to fill her slot, she took most of my nail business back to her sitting room.

I let it go. Whom you work with—and whom you trust—is just as important as carrying the right merchandise. You can't do it alone. You'll drive yourself crazy. But you can't do it with the wrong people, either. That woman clearly wasn't the right nail technician for Cheekys, so why worry?

(P.S. I worried anyway. I'm a worrier.)

During my years in business, I've hired a few accountants.
They all seem to look at things differently than I do. One in
particular was hired to keep track of inventory. When she saw
my invoices, she told me I was pricing my merchandise wrong.
She said I had to price everything at between two and a half
and three times what I paid for it.

I told her I didn't want to do that. She insisted. So I had to
let her go.

She wasn't wrong, I guess, because pricing that way is a
standard business practice. She probably learned that method
in school or in a book about how to run a retail operation. But
it isn't my standard business practice.

I work from the other end. Instead of letting my cost
determine my price, I ask myself, "What is this item worth?
How much would someone pay and still feel like they got a
good deal?"

Or to put it another way: "What price would I personally
be comfortable with, both as a seller *and* a buyer?"

(continued)

That's the price Cheekys charges. The perceived market value. The price that makes customers buy without thinking—and without thinking it's cheap.

Then I work backward from there. If I want to sell this item for twenty dollars, what can I afford to pay for it? Sometimes, at the wholesaler's price, my profit is less than twice my cost, but I bring the item in anyway, because I know my customers will love it. Other times, my profit margin is more than four times my cost. That doesn't mean I lower my price. My price is fair, right? Low cost relative to value just means Cheekys makes more money on each sale. A big part of my job is finding the highest-quality products from the most affordable sources.

Often, especially when I'm working with a new supplier, the numbers don't work. I can't buy the item at a cost that will allow me to offer my customers what I consider a fair price. If I can't negotiate my cost down to a reasonable level, I don't buy it. Even if I love it. Cheekys is a business, not a charity. There are many people I have wanted to do business with, but in the end the numbers made us part ways, not as partners but as friends.

They understand I'm not negotiating out of greed. I'm not interested in getting the lowest price no matter what. I want a fair price for a quality product. If we can all make money and still give the customer fair value, everybody wins. That's what I want: a system where everyone wins.

The accountant thought I was an incompetent woman who didn't understand pricing. She assumed I was making things up as I went along. She was wrong. I have a system. It's fixed and disciplined. It's just fixed from the other end. I always start with the customer, not myself.

CHAPTER 3

BE PRETTY

New Plymouth is a sleepy place. The two restaurants downtown barely serve lunch, and the Pilgrim Market only works one checkout and has only four aisles. The parking lot at Truckstop .com has more cars in it than the rest of the downtown combined, since the company has more than a hundred employees, but that building is a black hole. Once people go in, they seem to never come out. The main drag can get lively around the rodeo and the Big Nasty, an annual motorcycle race up the steep cliffs two miles east of town, but even on a Friday there are usually no more than four or five trucks parked in front of the Double Diamond and the other bar in town, The Club, half a block away. In the afternoon, it's common for there to be only one or two vehicles parked on Plymouth Avenue. You can sit on the bench in front of the senior center (rarely open) and see more logging trucks and farm equipment than cars. If anyone stops, it's usually for the ATM outside the world's smallest Zion's Bank branch.

This isn't an accident. It's the way people wanted it. For a long time, the citizens of New Plymouth fought anything that would bring in business, from new building permits to looser regulations. No changes, they said. Keep the present like the past. Even after the highway isolated the town, the citizens stayed stubborn. Even when the last generation of storeowners started to retire, nobody fought for the shops. When the Double Diamond went up for sale seven years ago, the owner of Truckstop.com tried to buy it. The owners wouldn't sell to him, though, because they knew he wanted to shut it down and retire the liquor license. He's Mormon, like half the town. He didn't approve of alcohol. That's New Plymouth: two places to hang out in the whole town, and most of the citizens wanted to shut one down. Thank goodness for Robin, the new owner. She's a pistol. It will take ten thousand crowbars to pry her out of her saloon.

So there was no red carpet rolled out for the opening of Cheekys. The idea that a small town—or any town—will support a business just because it's there is bull crap. That's not how the world works. I've lived in New Plymouth ten years, and I don't know half the people. There are hundreds who couldn't care less about Cheekys and a few dozen, at least, who don't know or can't remember we're here. I mean, eliminate the men and the children. That leaves maybe 600. Eliminate the Mormons. I love them, but most buy from other Mormons. That leaves 300 potential customers, and a majority of them aren't interested in what I'm selling.

Not the picture the gals on the Hub have in their heads when they think of Cheekys, I'm betting. It's cold and lonely in the retail business, even in Idaho.

That isn't to say people weren't friendly. They were. Many women loved having a new business in town, especially since my side of Plymouth Avenue was mostly vacant. They browsed my merchandise and chatted with me about the weather, the kids, the local gossip. They picked up items. "This is nice. Are you going to get it in other colors?"

No, I could barely afford that color.

"Maybe I'll come back and get it later."

I have an idea: why don't you buy it now? Please?

"Oh, I was looking for something just like that. I wish I'd known before I bought this other purse."

Well, I've been here the whole time.

I didn't say any of that, of course. I just breathed deep and remembered the words of Granny Dee, my dad's mom, whom I met for the first time at ten years old. Granny Dee always told me: *Be Pretty, Jessica.* She meant in the literal sense: do your hair, put on your makeup, dress well. Make yourself as beautiful as you can be. It drove her crazy that I played soccer and constantly had bruises and scratched-up knees. Granny Dee didn't believe a woman should leave the house without her face on, and that included a smile.

I hated that advice when I was a kid, but once I started selling for a living, I realized it was wise. I am not a glamorous person by nature. I'm thick and big in the chest, so I like loose-fitting clothes. I'm more comfortable in a bun than a 'do, and my hair has never been high or dyed. For Cheekys, though, I dressed nice. I knew I'd never be a popular girl. The in crowd wasn't inviting me for red wine. (Another thirty customers off the potentials list.) But I did my hair and tried my best with my makeup, and every time a woman walked in the door, no matter how desperate I was for a sale, I put on my face, meaning my smile.

"Hey, ladies," I said. "Welcome to Cheekys! How y'all doin' today?"

"Good, thanks!!"

"Can I help you with something?"

"Actually, you can. We were wondering if you could be a sponsor for..."

This is the bane of a small business: as soon as you open the doors, every person with a charitable cause will walk in and ask for a donation. It's just easier to approach a business, I guess, than a person (although the "business" and "person," in many cases, are really the same thing). Even in New Plymouth, there were dozens of fund-raisers and charities, especially for the schools, which in many ways were the pillars of the town. Everybody from the football team to 4H to the teachers needed support. There was the library, the baseball team, the elementary school carnival, the rodeo, our volunteer fire department. Justin volunteered as a fireman. His fireproof turnouts were so old the crotch was ripped out all the way to the knees. Trust me, you do not want to fight a fire in crotchless gear.

I wanted to help. I loved the community, and I didn't want them to think I was stuck up or selfish. But I had no money. When I said we started Cheekys with $7,000, that wasn't exactly true. We also had $100,000 in debt, because when Justin's partner declared bankruptcy, his business debt became ours.

We decided not to file for bankruptcy. I had a rat-ass childhood, but that's an important lesson my grandfather, Daddy Joe, taught me: *Keep your word, Jessica Dawn.* That's what he did when the Texas oil industry went bust in the 1980s and his plumbing business plunged into debt. His four partners declared bankruptcy, but Daddy Joe refused. He had recently taken his first (and only) trip overseas to Spain. Granny Dee loved it so much they retiled their kitchen in a Spanish style. Daddy Joe thought God was punishing him for that decadence.

"I don't think God would destroy Texas to teach you a lesson," I said—I was fourteen and a smartass—but Daddy Joe wouldn't budge.

"Either way, Jessica Dawn," he said, "I heard the message."

It took him twelve years to pay off those obligations, but he always believed he was a better man for seeing it through. For the rest of his life, he lived within his means, and he gave all that was left over to others once the bills were paid.

So Justin and I kept our word, even though debt is a hard road, since the end keeps moving away. We made every payment we could, but late fees and handling charges and fines kept us underwater. We ended up paying more than $300,000 on an original obligation of less than $75,000. So in 2011, considering debt versus assets and income, I suspect I was the poorest person in New Plymouth.

But I couldn't say no, could I? Not helping the 4H would get me on the wrong side of too many people too fast.

So here's what I did, and if you run a restaurant or storefront business, this one tip will probably save you a hundred times more than you paid for this book: I created a form.

Not a short form. A long form. Two full pages, too long to stand at my counter and fill out. The form asked about the charity, its goals, their personal involvement, and their personal goals. There was even an essay section. I never turned down anyone who asked for a donation. I just gave them the form.

If the person filled it out and brought it back, I gave them money, because they had proven their commitment. But 95 percent never brought it back. They didn't care enough to do the work, so why should I care enough to put their cause before my family's needs? And given their lack of effort, how could anyone blame me?

The long form is a business saver for more than donations. It's great for employee applications, too. You find out a person's commitment level real fast when you ask them to invest thirty minutes in writing. Sad but true.

Of course, there were Cheekys haters. There are always haters. It's even in the Bible. "Haters Gonna Hate, Proverbs 9:8," as it says on one of our shirts. (Or as the Bible puts it, "Reprove not a scorner.") One of the most common things I hear from other business owners is their frustration with that one relentless hater: in their town, in their family, sometimes even in themselves.

In my case, there was one woman in particular who spent a lot of time and energy trying to turn people against me. She talked about me behind my back. She painted me as an outsider to the older folks and as white trash to the moms. If she drove past my window and saw someone inside, or recognized a car parked out front, she called that person right then, *while they were in my store*, and made them super uncomfortable asking where they were. She told everyone I was a cheat, a lowlife, and a bad mom. She implied, at least once, that the power company regularly cut off power to my store for not paying my bills.

She had ammunition. Unfortunately, she had *so much* ammunition, because not long after we moved in next to the dairy, the allegations against me and my family started. We came home from our first family event, Hunter's middle school band concert, to find the sheriff's car in front of our house.

I looked at Justin. *Are we getting served? Why is the sheriff here after dark?*

I herded the kids toward the house, Hunter in a suit lugging a tuba, the other kids in nice sweaters and a dress, while Justin talked to the sheriff. I could see them out the window. They were talking, but it wasn't friendly, and there were no papers. I was confused. I sent the kids to their rooms and walked back out. The sheriff was grim. He told us he'd been contacted by Health and Welfare and needed to do a welfare check on our kids. We had to let him in our home. It was the law. And he was taking it very seriously. He looked like he wanted to bust our skulls. My heart was racing; I wanted to throw up. I didn't know what else to do but let him in.

When he walked in, he seemed genuinely surprised that our house was neat and clean. I took him to the pantry and kitchen first, because I assumed someone thought the kids weren't being fed. The sheriff had always gone to the kitchen first whenever he did a welfare check on me when I was a little girl. So I opened the door and showed him our huge pantry, packed with beautiful jars from my garden and stocked with food.

The sheriff chuckled. "You've been doin' some canning, huh?"

He went in every room and chatted with each of my kids. He checked their beds, all neatly made, and their closets, stuffed with clothes and costumes. He said he thought he was at the wrong address and apologized. He said he couldn't tell us what the accusations were, just that they were really bad and we needed to contact DHS in the morning.

A few days later, the sheriff was back. They had received another anonymous tip about child abuse. A few nights later, an anonymous caller claimed my children were sleeping in feces. Then it was sleeping in cages outside with the animals. Then that Justin and I were selling drugs and firearms out of the house, and then it got really bad—sexual abuse, physical abuse, and all kinds of awful stuff.

By the time I started Cheekys, these calls and visits had been happening *for more than two years*. I'm talking about dozens and dozens of calls and visits to my house by our small, overworked local sheriff department. The officers were apologetic. In fact, they were downright ashamed. "I'm sorry," they said, because they knew the tips were lies, "but it's the law. We're required to investigate every call. It's a shame we can't ask them to just do the Christlike thing and leave y'all alone."

It was harassment, but we had no recourse. The tips were anonymous. There was no way to prove, the sheriff said, who was doing it. But we had no doubts.

I had moved back to Idaho for Justin. I loved him, and I loved this state. But we had moved to Payette County, Idaho, because of Nick, my twins Jack and Sterling's biological father. I never loved him. I can say that now. Honestly, I'm not sure I ever liked him. My friends kept telling me to leave him. My boss referred to him a horse's ass. Even six-year-old Hunter thought he was a jerk.

When I got pregnant, Nick proved them right. He half-heartedly gave me a ring. Then I discovered that, without my knowledge or permission, he had pried the diamond out of the ring my ex-husband Ben had given me. He was planning to use that diamond to replace the fake in the ring he gave me. So I gave Nick his ring back until he got serious about being there for me and the baby. Instead, a few days after finding out I was carrying twins, he cleaned out his two drawers and toothbrush while I was at work and stopped answering my calls. Jack and Sterling were born ten weeks premature. Those little guys were in the NICU for forty days. Nick barely came to the hospital. And he sure wasn't paying for anything. He'd been dating two other women, I discovered, at the same time he was dating me, and he was still dating one of them. It was pretty clear to me that he didn't want to be a part of our lives.

The twins were a blessing from God, and not just because they showed me some hard truths about Nick. I was twenty-seven. I was crushing it in the car business, working six days a week, ten hours a day. I had a nice house, a maid, and a nanny. Hunter was in a private Christian school across the street from my dealership. I was successful, but I wasn't living quite right. I was drinking bourbon with my girlfriends two to three times a week. I was going to the local dive bars to hustle a little pool. I guess I was living out my foolish younger years, the ones I missed when I was working full-time and raising my baby boy.

Don't get me wrong. I made some great memories. Hunter and I danced together in our little house all the time. I introduced him to Dr. Dre and created his lifelong love of hip-hop and underground rap. Trisha never partied with me at the bars. She was my steady older friend, my best babysitter, and it was the nights with her and Hunter and her son, Ryan, laughing and eating home-cooked meals, playing board games and shooting the breeze that I value to this day. And yet, there I was, getting knocked up by a guy who lived in an RV, drove a freaking dirt bike like it was his primary vehicle...and wasn't nice to my son! What in the world was I thinking?!

The pregnancy showed me what I cared about. The money wasn't making me happy. Neither were the evenings in bars. I wanted love. I wanted a family. I wanted God's grace in my life. I found that the moment I felt Jack and Sterling kicking in my womb, and then I found it again two months after they were born with Justin.

We met at the Dodge dealership where we both worked, me in sales and him in the service department. I told him on the first date I was a single mom with three boys, two of them ten weeks old and barely out of the hospital. To my surprise, his response was, "I love babies!"

He might be an Idaho farm boy with a big ol' pickup truck, but puppies, kittens, ducklings, even monkeys...if it's small and cute, Justin loves it. And like a true farm boy, he fears no poop. Ladies, if you want a real man to do the dirty work, marry a farm boy.

A couple dates later, I told Justin I was moving to Texas. I felt alone in Idaho, I told him, and I needed to go home to my father's family.

"When you leaving?" he asked.

"In two weeks."

He paused, but only for a second. "I'm not opposed to moving there."

"Look," I said, "I really, and I mean *really*, like you, Justin, but I'm sorry, I won't live with a man I'm not married to." I'd learned that lesson. It's too easy to walk out when you haven't made a promise to each other and God.

"Well," Justin said, "what are you doing on Sunday?"

My grandpa, Daddy Joe, always said: "Love comes with time, Jessica Dawn, but if you like someone, you can partner with 'em." And I liked Justin a lot. We wanted the same things, we went well together, and I could work with that. I guess God had a plan for me all along.

We were married on Sunday. We were moving on Tuesday. On Monday, with his mother's prodding, Nick filed an injunction to keep me from taking the twins out of state—along with a request for a paternity test, because he still hadn't publicly acknowledged the children were his despite my putting him on their birth certificates. *Really?* I thought. *Now? After all those months of pushing us away?*

The judge granted me permission to move. He gave Nick

supervised visitation. He wasn't allowed to see the boys alone. We lived in Texas for two years; Nick came with his mother to see the boys only a handful of times.

When Justin and I decided to move back to Idaho, I tried to make peace with Nick. As much as I distrusted him, I thought my sons would benefit from a good relationship with their father. So I agreed to share custody, although I remained their primary guardian, an arrangement that was working great with my first husband, Hunter's father, Ben. I agreed to send them to school in Payette County, close to where both Nick's parents and Justin's family lived. I thought I was doing the right thing. I thought that would create a healthy situation for everyone.

It didn't. From the moment we moved to Payette County, people aligned with Nick and his mother, many of whom I'd never even met, and spread rumors about me. They or their friends made the calls to Health and Welfare alleging every abuse you could think of. Within a year of my opening Cheekys, Nick demanded an emergency custody hearing. They had "heard the accusations," they said. They were concerned. Who would say such terrible things if they weren't true? They had to get the boys away from me, immediately, for their safety!

The judge not only denied the request, he had their testimony and all the documents sealed to protect my children. The accusations against me and my family were so heinous and unsupported, they would have harmed all four children if they became public knowledge.

"Can this please stop?" I begged Nick. "I don't care what you say about me or what I have to do. Please don't do this to the twins. Don't do this to my other children. Can't we come to an agreement for their sakes?"

He looked down at me. "You shouldn't have gone to Texas," he said.

Well, if you'd given me any support, I wouldn't have had to!

The anonymous tips didn't stop. And the accusations didn't stay private. They were everywhere, available to anyone who wanted to listen. Those were the rumors the popular women in New Plymouth heard about me. That's what some people chose to believe. It wasn't necessarily malicious. I had a good customer who drove in from the other side of Ontario, over by the big butte. One day, I mentioned that I knew someone over that way. As soon as I said it, I knew it was a mistake, and sure enough...

"Oh, who do you know?"

I mentioned the twins. She knew them. "I'm their mom," I said.

"Oh. I didn't know Nick was married." She thought I was his new wife. "I am so sorry about all that trouble. I heard their biological mother is strung out on drugs and living in a car."

"Nope," I said sadly. "That's me. And I'm not."

That's why it hurt so much when the woman in New Plymouth spread that gossip in my town. I think she considered me competition to a little home-based business she ran. I think she wanted to hurt Cheekys, but the real damage was to my family. People turned on Hunter, who was about eleven at the time. They thought he was a bad kid from a bad family, and I believe they subconsciously started to see everything he did in that light.

Life became hard for him after that. Real hard. And Jack and Sterling…it hurts me to think what they've been through, and that includes me writing this honestly about my relationship with their father.

That's why I never insult other stores. I never try to hurt anyone's business, and I definitely never attack other owners personally. Those women aren't my competition; they are mothers, wives, sisters, and daughters. They have families. They are trying to find love, happiness, and financial security, just like me.

I cried over the harassment. I'm not ashamed of that. I cry when I'm hurt, so I cried a lot. I prayed every night for it to stop.

But I never spoke out. I never made public what was happening, because I didn't want to drag the twins into a public fight. "Reprove not the scorner," as the Bible says.

Or in Granny Dee's words: *Be Pretty*. She didn't just mean my face. She meant *Be Nice*. Granny Dee knew my childhood was hard. I was a hated child. I know many children feel that way, but in my case, it was true. My mother was so notorious that the other mothers wouldn't allow their children to be friends with me. They pointed to me on the street, even when I was six or seven years old, and said, "You stay away from her, you hear?" I only had one bike my whole life, and it was stolen. My mother and I were mugged at gunpoint in our front yard. Someone killed my dog by hanging him from the tree outside my bedroom window. I think it was the man I was forced to call my father, but I'm not sure. The older children were always threatening to do it. For a year, kids in my neighborhood threw their leftover lunches and drinks at me every day when I got off the bus.

I was a little girl of prayer. I prayed all the time, although I have no idea were I learned that. My mother was a sad and selfish addict, champagne and inhalants mostly, and she didn't teach me anything good. But I was a little girl desperate for a friend, any friend, and God was there. I was the little girl who forced herself to smile into the bathroom mirror when she was alone just to prove she could. Later, when Granny Dee told me to smile, it was easy, because I'd already trained myself to do it. Even when I was hurting... even when I felt like I was dying... I forced myself to smile.

I didn't cry by the time I met Granny Dee, because after a while children just don't cry anymore. But she would see me with whatever look I had on my face when it was too much, and she would grab me sort of desperately and say, "Be pretty, Jessica. Be pretty."

She meant, *Be Strong*. No matter what they say or do to you, girl, put on your smile. Be kind. Let them know you're a lady, and ladies stand tall. They never bend, and they sure as hell don't break.

I'm not sure that was good advice. It may actually be terrible advice. You can't hold your fear and pain alone, and you can't keep silent about the things that are done to you.

But what do you expect? Granny Dee weighed ninety pounds, drank a suitcase of Natural Light every day—that's a twenty-four-pack of cans to those of you who don't shop at the gas station—and not once did I see her drunk. She was hard and unbreakable, like she thought a woman had to be to survive.

There was a piece of wisdom in her advice, though: that if I could smile despite the circumstances, then I was in control of me, my future, and my heart. A smile meant the hurt didn't own me. I believed that, and that truth saw me through brutal times. It worked as a life philosophy for many years.

But here's an even more important truth: You will achieve nothing by getting in arguments with the people who treat you wrong. You will only lower yourself, waste your energy, and make mistakes. If you are fighting them, you can't focus on yourself. And you have to believe in yourself. You have to be clear-eyed about what you are doing. That doesn't mean criticism doesn't hurt. It does. That means you can't let it change who you are. You can't let that pain own you or take you away from the people that need you.

So I stayed pretty (as best I could). I not only kept quiet, I watched for opportunities to prove myself. When one gossiping woman's son made a traveling sports team, I went to her and said, "Congratulations. I know they have a fund-raiser every year. If you send your son by the store, I'd be happy to contribute."

I did that four times, with four different women. It didn't really work. Years later, my daughter, Addy, who was a baby when all this started, was bullied in the first grade. When I asked her why, Addy told me the girl said, "Your mom stole my mom's store."

Being pretty won't change a woman like that. It won't change those consequences. It's still worth it. It's always worth it to be true to your best self.

But it's not easy, especially when you're struggling. As I said, my total income for 2012 was $43,000—and that was *before* expenses. Justin and I sold almost everything we owned just to stay afloat. Every time Justin managed to round himself up a tractor or a tool—his dad worked at the local John Deere dealership, so Justin came by his love of tractors honestly—it was sold to make ends meet. That husband of mine sold every single "toy" and tool to get us by, and that man loves his tools.

That's stressful. It's a marriage crusher. Justin and I argued more the year we opened Cheekys than we have ever argued before or since. I had a little storeroom/office behind the counter (also known as the homework spot), and Justin and I would go at it in there, where no one could hear. It wasn't just about the store; it was about the house, the school, the finances, the rumors, and that sad, sorry mini-tractor someone missed so very much.

One day, after a particularly heated exchange, I came storming out to find a teenage girl standing at the counter. We had a bell on the door, but neither Justin nor I had heard it. I must have been giving him hell.

"Oh," I said, but thinking, *Oh, shit* as I plastered that pretty smile on my face. "Hi, there. I am so sorry. What can I help ya with?"

"Do you have an application for a job or anything?" she asked.

I laughed. "Seriously?!" *Did I hear her right? Is she deaf?* "You want to work here after what you just heard?"

"Ah," she said with a smile and a wave of her hand. "My mom yells at my dad like that, too."

I am sure Justin was in our little closet thinking the same thing I was: *Please don't tell everyone what just happened.* But the girl just stood there, staring at me like she wasn't bothered, so I handed her a long application. "Well, if you can handle that," I joked, "then I should probably hire you."

And I did. Her name was Morgan. She was fifteen, a sophomore in high school, and she was Cheekys' first employee.

Now all I needed to do was figure out how I could afford to pay her.

CHAPTER 4

FACEBOOK AND RODEOS:

A BROKE GIRL'S GUIDE TO MARKETING

I hired Morgan because she happened to walk in the door but also because I needed help. I realized how much help the day I felt in my gut something was wrong, so I closed the store to go home and check on Justin. He was lying in bed in the middle of the afternoon with tears in his eyes. Justin is a farm boy. He goes to bed about eight-thirty and wakes up at the crack of dawn. He can build, haul, raise, or fix just about anything, and he never sits still. (The closest he comes is about an hour in the evening when the only thing moving is his arm, doing a twelve-ounce curl with his red beer.) He was always working two or three small construction jobs around the valley to help pay our bills, and getting more jobs out of those, because like I said, everybody loves him.

At night, he answered calls for the volunteer fire department and EMT service. Our fire department was five volunteers back then, so Justin was out on just about every call.

One night, a semi shredded a tire on I-84 and the sparks from the metal-on-asphalt started brush fires for a mile. Lightning strikes set the brush prairie on fire fifteen or twenty times a year. Often, the first two people on the scene were Justin and Alan, a local farmer who had served as New Plymouth's volunteer fire chief for twenty-five years. Justin worked a deadly car accident involving local teens (the worst nightmare), a farm accident involving neighbors (heartbreaking), and the removal of a dead body so decayed they had to wrap it in the carpet to keep it from falling apart.

He was never traumatized. Nothing made him blink, until he unknowingly handled a woman with a deadly contagious disease without proper protection, and he quit being an EMT the next day. He cried for joy when Addy was born. He's laughed so hard he cried plenty of times. But I never saw Justin truly break down until that day in our room.

"I can't do it anymore," he said. "I'm sorry, Jessi. I don't know how to stop feeling bad."

We were deep in old debt. We were struggling with Cheekys. Nick and his mom were starting a formal action to challenge our custody of the twins, and that meant time and money and worry that we might lose our sons.

What broke Justin, though, was his biological mother.

I'm going to keep saying biological, because Justin has a real mom. She married his dad when he was nine, she raised him, and she's awesome. She's Grandma Roberts.

His biological mom walked out on the family when Justin was four. He didn't see her again until right before he married me, but we welcomed her into our life. Dinah moved with us to Texas, and Granny Dee financed and owner-carried a loan on the little house Justin and I remodeled for her. Dinah was not a pleasant person, and she hated me. She hated both her daughters-in-law, in fact. We still moved her back to Idaho with us. She was a self-proclaimed bookkeeper, so we let her keep the books for Justin's company, because finally having his biological mom in his life was important to him.

I understood. My mom was toxic, but I struggled for sixteen years to preserve our relationship after my dad finally rescued me at eleven. No matter what mom did to me, I thought God had commanded me to love her. I thought it was my spiritual duty to be an obedient daughter, and I thought being obedient meant giving her everything. I finally cut her off when the twins were born, for the sake of my children.

We didn't realize how dangerous Dinah was until she took more than $20,000 from the company. This was at the end, after Justin's partner filed for bankruptcy and the wheels were coming off. She and her husband went to the Oregon coast, ate fancy meals at expensive hotels, and gambled the money away—when we had four children to feed!

When we called her on it, she sought out Nick. She wanted leverage back into our lives, but when we didn't take her back, she became our tormentor. She made harassing phone calls. She accused us of drug dealing, child abuse, and so much worse. We had the same attorney Justin's father had had for his divorce. He told us, "These are the same accusations, in practically the same words, that she used against him."

Now, if there is any man in this world nicer than Justin, it's his dad. He's a slightly shorter, slightly heftier, more soft-spoken version of Sam Elliott, right down to the mustache, and Sam Elliott is a freaking American hero. Cheekys sells a beer cozy with his mustache on it that says on the bottom, "Tip your can to Sam," that's how much we love him.

There was no truth to Dinah's accusations, then or now. It was vengeance, nothing more. She wanted to destroy her own son, and all he'd ever tried to do was love her.

It broke Justin. It truly broke his heart. Shortly after I found him crying at home, he had to be hospitalized for depression and anxiety. Many men in Justin's position, especially small-town men, would become hostile, embarrassed, or even violent in that situation. Or they'd deny the problem. Justin embraced his treatment.

"Yep," he admits whenever anyone asks. "I lost it there for a minute. But they gave me a few pills to take, a nice break, some therapy, and now I'm right as rain."

And he was. Justin was back to himself in a matter of weeks. But it made me mad, seeing a good man pushed like that. Seeing my kids hurt by false accusations. Seeing old debt piling up because we did the right thing and didn't file for bankruptcy. The mountain in front of us seemed like Everest, and I knew there was only one way over it—growing Cheekys fast enough and strong enough to support us all.

That meant marketing. No business can grow without marketing. I've seen successful boutique owners on the Internet tell other women just starting out, "Oh, I just grew my business to a couple million dollars on word of mouth." The implication being their store is so amazing, and customers love them sooooo much, that their success was practically effortless... and if that's not happening for you, it's because you're just not as awesome as they are.

Lies, lies, lies.

You have to market your company *and* yourself. You have to market *constantly* and *relentlessly*. But good news: there are hundreds of ways to do that.

In Boise, I founded an advertising agency after running ad campaigns at several car dealerships. My ads were so famous around town, especially my funky billboards, that I won several awards. I was one of the youngest recipients ever chosen for Idaho's top "40 Under 40" businesspeople. But that work was for dealerships with substantial marketing budgets. Cheekys didn't have a dime. How could I tell the world I was here with a marketing budget of zero dollars?

I decided to try Facebook. No bullshit about my reason: 1) it was free, and 2) I had heard of it. Turned out to be one of the best decisions I ever made, because I started on Facebook at the perfect time. Not perfect because of where Facebook was as a company, but because of where I was as a company. Broke, eager, desperate, and thirsting for knowledge.

People often ask how to get started on Facebook, since I've been successful there. I tell them it's simple: read Facebook's tutorial on setting up a business page. It's free. It's straightforward. Do not pay hundreds or thousands of dollars for a class. Facebook wants you to have a business page on its platform, so it provides everything you need to get started. If you can't figure it out after their tutorial, read a book. They cost about twenty dollars.

Once you're set up, start posting. Don't try to be perfect; no business ever succeeded because of one perfect photo, or even a hundred. It's the volume that matters. You have to post regularly, so there's always new information. Customers have to get to know who you are, trust you, and depend on you, and that only happens when you put yourself out to the public again and again. The posts can be photos of merchandise. They can be events. They can be special prices. The important thing is to post—and watch what works.

Today, I update my page, Cheekys Boutique, every few hours. When I started, I tried to update every few days. That wasn't easy, because I didn't have much material (or so I thought). I had a tiny store. I had one part-time high school employee. I only bought new items every couple of weeks, because I couldn't afford to do it more often.

So I got creative. If I had five purses, I photographed them on my nicest display. Then I moved them to a different corner of the store, shuffled the order, and posted them again. Sometimes, I showed the same purse five times in a week, in five different photos with five different accessories beside it. Since Addy was always in the store, I had her model my children's items. I have old posts of her wearing tutus, fairy wings, and a tiger-striped jumper that is super cute, but I don't even remember carrying it.

It was all very amateurish, complete with my overenthusiastic personal comments, too many emojis, and weak attempts at humor. (Um, okay, yes, I still do all those things, but at least the pictures have gotten better.) Everything you post on Facebook remains in your history unless you delete it, so I often look at those early photos and shake my head. The store layout was crowded, with barely enough room for a stroller to make it down the aisles. My displays were cluttered. I took photos with my iPhone, so they were often out of focus or flared, or half a random foot was sticking in from the side. (I still take my photos with an iPhone, but both the phones and I have greatly improved since 2012.)

Sometimes, when a fellow boutique owner is down about her website or Facebook page, I tell her, "Go into my history. Seriously. Look at what I was doing when I started. It will make you feel a lot better."

You have to make mistakes! That's the magic, girls. You have to jump in and go for it. You'll get better; it's called practice. Lots of boutique owners delete their early history, but why? I am not at all embarrassed of how I started, because I know I started at the bottom. Those old photos are treasures. They feature long-time customers. They feature items with great stories behind them. Every photo brings back a memory, and even the worst are fun for a laugh. Little Addy in fairy wings? That's precious. She's eleven going on thirty now, and I miss my little girl. My daughter in fairy wings to promote my business? That's priceless.

None of those lame photos killed Cheekys, after all.

In fact, they worked. My Facebook followers picked up every week, and soon people were driving from other parts of the valley to check out my store. Why? Because what I posted was authentic. You can be as professional as you want; you can hire photographers and models and feature gauzy backgrounds of beautiful trees, but you're never going to be in the same league as Target or Cabela's. Your best online life is being exactly who you are in real life. If that's goofy, so be it (up to a point). If that's small town or rural, God bless you. If you have a regular woman's body, be proud of it. In the end, your best customers are the people out there who are most like you.

In other words: Do NOT fake it until you make it.

By all means, be at your best. Photograph your products on nice displays. Clean up the clutter. Think about the lighting. Take ten photos of your daughter in a tutu and choose the best one. *Be professional.* I'm amazed by some of the stuff I see in the background of photos. Your unmade bed? Your unwashed laundry? Really? Get it together. But never lie about who you are, because who you are—as the storeowner and person who decides what is sold—is your greatest asset. Even if you don't own a business, for goodness sake, just be yourself. As weird as it sounds, it's often your screw-ups that people most identify with and admire.

From the start, I took the photos. My models were real customers. The location was Cheekys or New Plymouth, not a gauzy field or a metropolitan hot spot. I wrote the way I talked: fast, loud, and not as funny as I thought. Even though I rarely showed my face (I'm shy about my looks), I showed the real person behind Cheekys. A mom. A wife. A woman with an eye for merchandise and a strong connection to rural Idaho and the people who lived here.

Looking back, I might not have been 100 percent honest, because a lot of people arrived expecting more than my store. So many women walked in, looked around, and said the same thing. "Oh, this is a lot smaller than I thought it would be."

That's when I walked out from behind the counter smiling, in full *Be-Pretty* mode with my selling shoes on. "Yeah, it's pretty crowded in here, huh? But I like to say you can walk through, crawl through, and tiptoe through and see something new each time! Can I grab ya a bottle of Coke for a quarter while ya browse?"

My sales kept getting better. I would never sell ice to Inuits, but I was good at selling quality clothes, purses, and accessories to Payette Valley women and, occasionally, their husbands. If I got a woman in Cheekys, I could sell her, because once she started looking around, she realized the store really did match what she loved on Facebook. We did haircuts. We did nails. But even without the extras, I could keep a woman in the store for an hour, and, usually, she left feeling she'd received good value for her long drive. That's how you keep old customers and make new ones. Give them an experience better than they expected.

I was still broke, though, so I decided to take Cheekys on the road. There's not much going on in rural Idaho in the winter. Sometimes, the snow is so bad you can't get out the driveway. The highway to Portland often closes for weeks at a time because the rolling, ice-covered hills cause semis to jackknife and crash into each other. During the winter of 2016–2017, the snowfall was so high the UPS guy couldn't get to New Plymouth for weeks. Believe me, that was a disaster.

But spring not only brings warm weather and great fishing, it brings the rodeo. There's at least one rodeo a week through the fall, including a minor-league event in New Plymouth, and they rent space to vendors. This was prime boutique territory. There were booths selling ropes, $250 cowboy hats, pearl-snap Western shirts, and thousand-dollar saddles, but most sold women's apparel. It wasn't flea market quality, either. These ladies had chrome trailers, fancy barns, and complicated get-ups. One woman always paid a man to pull her decked-out double-size trailer into position, then paid a crew to set up her merchandise. She had a rodeo queen air: big blond hair, tight body, the works. She never broke a sweat or a manicured fingernail. She was that rich girl on her third husband, the popular girl in high school all grown up.

Then here come Justin and I in our Yukalade, with all our stuff strapped to the roof like the Clampetts. We'd spill out with our kids—the twins were often with Nick, but Hunter and Addy always came with us—and our tent. That's right. Everyone else had a trailer. Cheekys had a tent. It was a hot mess, like actually hot and actually a mess, bought from Costco and leftover from one of Justin's construction jobs. It took two adults and two kids about two hours to wrestle it into shape.

Most rodeos were weekend-long events, so I'd bring half the store. I only left enough for Morgan to stay open while I was gone. Hard to believe I left a teenager in charge of Cheekys, but our hair stylist Promise helped run the place when I was away, and Morgan was tough. She had a lot of confidence for a high school student, and she took pride in my trust. She wouldn't let me down. And besides, this was New Plymouth. I never worried about crime. Late-night scuffles at the Double Diamond? Heck, yeah. But not robbery. My biggest worry was that Morgan's boyfriend would distract her. Morgan always fell too hard for her latest crush.

Those weekend shows were hard work, but they were our family vacations, too. While I manned the booth, Justin took the kids out: carnival rides in Twin Falls, face painting at the Apple Blossom Festival, and of course the rodeo. Why live in rural Idaho if you don't love the rodeo? I mean, where else can your kid chase down, tackle, and then keep a live chicken! I loved the excited stories the kids told me over late-night fair food dinners, the free trinkets Addy was so good at rounding up, and the "adventure" of sleeping in the Yukalade together because money was too tight for a hotel.

Sales were slow, though. Too slow. At half the shows, I barely covered expenses. I told myself it was marketing. I was exposing the Cheekys brand to thousands of women in my target demographic. And I was clicking up followers on Facebook. Even after slow shows, there were special orders through our page. But it wasn't enough. Nick was suing me for custody of the twins. I needed money, not buzz.

The problem dawned on me one day when I looked at the long line of women's boutiques in the blazing hot parking lot of one of the biggest rodeos in Idaho and realized most of us were carrying the same merchandise. That's because we were all buying from the same ten or twelve large wholesale websites, and those guys didn't give a damn. They would sell to every store in your town if they could. If you had $150 for an initial order, that was enough, no questions asked. At a certain point, selling their products was nothing more than offering a lower price than all the other boutiques.

That's a losing game, and I didn't want to play it. I was always checking the local festivals, looking for unique merchandise. I was always asking local craftsmen and women to make changes so Cheekys products were better (in my opinion) than what they sold elsewhere. There just wasn't enough of that stuff. So I started looking farther away and discovered wholesalers had their own markets in big cities like Atlanta, Los Angeles, and New York. One of the largest was the Market Center in Dallas, Texas. They had a three-day apparel and accessories show four times a year.

I couldn't afford a plane ticket to Texas, so I took the Yuka-lade. It was nice and roomy, but I wanted more space. If I was driving 1,600 miles to a trade show, I needed to bring home a lot of merchandise. I couldn't afford a trailer, so I looked around New Plymouth for options. The blacksmith who worked out of a garage around the corner from Cheekys had an old U-Haul. (Yes, he's a real blacksmith. He makes and fits horseshoes for ranchers. We really are cowboys here.) I asked if I could borrow it for a week. He said I could, as long as I stayed in Payette County. The thing was held together with duct tape, and he wasn't sure it would last on the open road.

"Oh, I'll take real good care of it," I said. "I promise."

I'm sorry, Jerry. I really am. It was just a little white lie.

So that's how I ended up hauling a taped-together trailer

behind a ten-year-old half-Yukon, half-Escalade on a three-day drive. Along the way, I posted short video messages on the Cheekys Facebook page. Me with one hand on the wheel and the desert flying by in the background, saying into my iPhone, "Hey, girls, I made it to Utah. I'm going to find some good stuff for y'all. Stay ready," that kind of thing. I'm not comfortable with myself; I don't like being in front of the camera. Those were the last posts to show my face for almost five years.

I had slightly more than 1,000 Facebook followers by then. I remember, because I was so excited. I watched the counter for weeks, and when I finally made it to 1,000, I celebrated. I thought I'd hit the big time. Today, Cheekys has more than 400,000 followers. I know that intimidates girls just starting out, and I know I keep hitting this point again and again, but it's important: Don't look at where I am now. Look at where I *was*, because we all start with nothing but our dreams. Finding an audience means building an audience, and that takes time. Right now, Cheekys adds 15,000 followers a month, but it took me *an entire year* of working at it every day to get to 1,000. So if your followers are still in the hundreds, or even the double digits, keep posting. Keep working. Keep getting better.

It's a big world out there, and nothing demonstrated that to me more than Dallas. I don't mean the city. I'm a Texas girl; I knew Houston and Dallas. I love big cities, and even giant ones like Los Angeles. To visit, not to live in, of course. I'll take my Idaho farmhouse over a penthouse any day of the week.

The place that awed me was the Dallas Market Center: five million square feet of retail space, in four interconnected buildings. The entire complex, and I mean every inch, was taken up by wholesalers. It was like a mall that never ended. Some showrooms were big, some small, some elaborate, some bare as bones, and some so far down side corridors you only ended up there when you were lost. There were millions of items to choose from and wholesalers from all over the world. Why, I wondered, had I limited myself to Idaho for so long? Fear? Money? Both? Well, there was no looking back now.

I was on the hunt for very specific items in a very specific style: affordable, well-made clothing and accessories, for rural and small-town women, with a Western feel. I was confident in my ability to find great items in that category. Still, the selection was jaw-dropping. How could I rake through a million choices (not an exaggeration) without losing my mind? And how could I stretch my tiny budget *ju-u-u-st* far enough?

I started snapping photos and posted them to the Cheekys Facebook page.

"What do you girls think of this shirt?"

"I love this belt. What about you?"

To my surprise, a few women immediately posted back. Then, when other women saw those comments, they posted, too. Soon, we had a dialogue going. I'd post my favorite items, and followers would comment on them. One woman wrote under a photo of a pair of earrings: "I love those. Can I buy them now?"

Hmm. Why not?

I private messaged to ask if she was serious, and if so, what price was she thinking? We negotiated for a half second and came to an agreement. She paid up front with a credit card, and

I bought the earrings. Actually, I bought a couple pairs, because if she liked it, and I liked it, I needed it at Cheekys.

Soon, I was making sales to other women. My Facebook page was like a private shopper/running commentary on the Dallas Market (or "Market," as we call wholesale shows in the business), and I loved it. I was so excited I walked around taking photos after the shops had closed for the night, trying not to catch the glare off their windows so no one would know I wasn't inside. First thing the next morning, I was back, buying items my Facebook followers liked and taking more photos.

By the end of two days, I had everything bought and more than half of it sold. It took an extra day to drive home, because the trailer was so stuffed I worried it would pop if I topped sixty-one miles per hour. I probably had a thousand items, much more than I could have afforded if I hadn't been pre-selling as I went along, and the last thing I needed was for it to be all over the freeway! I thought those items would last Cheekys six months, but I was wrong. While I was on the road, women who had participated in the Dallas conversations told their friends about Cheekys, or maybe followers who hadn't visited our page over the weekend came back and discovered what they had missed, because, long story short, by the time I hit New Plymouth, I had sold 99 percent of everything in the trailer.

I thought. *This is it, Jessi. You're onto something here. You could build a sustainable business out of this.*

The "this" in that thought wasn't the Dallas Market; it was customer interaction and community.

I make a lot of my own merchandise now, and, yes, most of it is produced overseas. Some people get bent out of shape about that, and I understand. American manufacturing has had a hard run. Many people, including many people I know, have been hurt when factories closed.

So I'm sympathetic when people tell me: "I won't buy anything made in China. That's why I pay more for Montana West."

Well, I hate to break it to you, ladies, but Montana West is owned by a Korean-American who manufactures mostly overseas. Please understand: I'm not against the company. I know the owner. He's a good guy. But I'm pretty sure he's never stepped foot in Montana.

And it's not just them. Almost everybody manufactures overseas, even companies that market their products with pictures of mountains, horses, and vintage Americana. Yes, even some of the ones who say they're American made. Look closer. They're not. They're *American designed.*

(continued)

Want to know something worse? Most of that "hair on hide" you see on furniture, rugs, and just about everywhere else these days? It's from China, and it's not cow.

It's pony.

That's why I'm *very* careful when sell anything "hair on hide."

Remember how I said I determine a fair price for my customers, then work backward to see if my cost makes the item feasible to carry? Sadly, I rarely hit my price target with American-made items. A blank t-shirt made in America costs me eight or nine dollars. That's my wholesale cost before design, ink, labor, marketing, and overhead. A blank t-shirt from my contact overseas costs less than five dollars. For a retailer like Cheekys, that's the difference between being in business and being broke.

And most of the time, the shirts from overseas are better quality. That's the roughest part for patriotic retailers like me. I gave a larger order to an American manufacturer in late 2016; I thought I might be able to make it work, even at the extra cost. The shirts came in stretched out, poorly stitched, with the wrong tags. I had to eat that cost, because I will never sell poor-quality merchandise. That's a broken promise I can't afford.

I know there are good arguments against overseas manufacturing, but I'm careful. No child labor, no excessive pollution, nothing like that. I'd like to buy American, but in the end, Cheekys is about putting *customers* first and putting food on the table of as many families as possible.

I know who I work with overseas. They're good people. And you know what? They have families to feed and care for, too.

So I put my process right on my tags:

- AMERICAN DESIGNED.
- FOREIGN MANUFACTURED.
- NO YANKEES WERE HARMED IN THE MAKING OF THIS SHIRT.

CHAPTER 5

NO BIG BREAKTHROUGHS...

JUST FIFTY SMALL ONES

Dallas wasn't a "breakthrough." It didn't suddenly make Cheekys successful. I often think of that scene in *Forrest Gump* where Forrest says, "Have a nice day," and snap, a million people are wearing a smiley-face shirt.

That's how so many entrepreneurs think the world works. We're so used to hearing about "the big idea" that we assume that's what will happen to us. We struggle, we struggle, and then, bam, something hits and we make a million dollars.

Yeah, success doesn't work that way.

Except in rare instances, nobody succeeds because of one evolutionary leap. It takes years of little increases. You have to keep looking ahead and making the next positive step, and the next one, and the next.

Dallas helped. It was important, no doubt. I made enough money from that trip to breathe easier for the next three or four months. But all the other small steps we took that year helped too, like the twenty-four-by-eight pink barn Justin built for the rodeos. Like I said, my man loves his projects. The barn screwed together onsite, so we transported the pieces on a flatbed trailer, borrowed from his dad, with all our merchandise piled on top. It was a bear to assemble. The sides were wooden slats, so they were heavy, and it's a hard to hold two heavy walls in place while you power screw. It wasn't until the next summer that Justin's friend Hoot said, "Well, hell, Justin, why don't you just build the damn thing permanently onto the trailer?"

So look for the pink Cheekys barn, ladies! We might be hauling it soon to a location near you.

After that, I used my Dallas windfall to buy a screen printer from a going-out-of-business sale. I had always wanted to print my own shirts; this was the first time it seemed affordable. *Barely* affordable, but that's the thing about a small business, you have to reinvest. Every time Justin and I worked up a little stash of money, we invested it into growing Cheekys. There's no other way, because a business is like a shark, you either keep going forward or you drown. If you can't embrace that, you're not an entrepreneur. That's okay. Just don't lie to yourself about what you want.

So Justin drove two and a half hours to pick up the press, then installed it in a metal storage unit behind Cheekys that we rented for $250 a month. It was a four-over-four manual press, meaning it had four stations. You pushed one color through a screen, then moved the shirt to the next station to add the second color. So for full color, you had to line up and press each shirt perfectly four times. This wasn't the newest press on the block, so nothing was quite square, and the shed had no water and only limited power. It was another hot, sticky mess.

It was also a turning point for the company. Ever since, I've been moving Cheekys away from being a seller of other people's products toward making and distributing our own designs, which you'll learn about later.

And it finally, *finally*, gave Justin a place in the company. He was never happy buying and selling women's apparel. I mean, he's a sensitive guy, but not *that* sensitive. He owns eighty-three wrenches and a pickup truck! That's part of the reason I kept coming up with building projects: to give poor Justin work he enjoyed.

Now he had his own playground. While I worked on shirt designs with a graphics company in Nampa, a little town outside Boise, Justin taught himself to print. That meant figuring out where to buy ink and screens. How much ink to apply. How to line up the shirts on each pressing station. What material held ink best. It turned out he needed a dryer to cure the ink, so he found one on Craigslist. Then he had to rework the electrical box at the shed and reconfigure the machinery. Any time Justin gets to reconfigure machinery, he's in heaven.

But, oh, my God, was it a disaster! Shirts were coming out crooked, missing colors, looking like 3-D photos without the glasses on because the bushings were misaligned. It was summer, so the shed was boiling. It was so hot some days the ink would dry and clog the screens. Or it smeared when Justin's man-sweat (ugh) dripped all over it.

The first shirt we designed and printed said, "Every girl loves a dirty cowboy." The second shirt said: "Cowboys Lie" (because they do, at the least the ones at the rodeos). I wasn't a designer, but I was bossy with the graphics folks in Nampa. I knew what I wanted: "Cowboys Lie" with two stars, one in front of the words and one at the end. And only one color, since Justin still couldn't press multiple colors correctly.

He still screwed up! I wanted a hundred shirts for the Caldwell Nights Rodeo, the biggest event in the lower Payette Valley, and Justin must have pressed three hundred shirts to get a hundred right. Of course, that's when I realized there was an even bigger problem with my design. Those two stars at the ends of "Cowboys Lie"... they were smack on the tatas. They were like two big searchlight beams: *Hey, boys, look at these!*

I thought, *Okay, stupid, you need to try on every design before going into production.*

I sold them anyway, with an honest warning. I had more than a thousand dollars and a month of work into them, what else could I do? Turns out the local bartenders, who are mostly women, loved them. "Cowboys Lie" made their tips go up. Yes, I mean their customer tips. And yes, I realize that doesn't exactly advance the cause of women, but at least we could all pay some bills, right?

Cheekys actually ended up selling a ton of the star-spangled "Cowboys Lie" design—on scooped tank tops. In that context, it worked.

"Cowboys Lie" was definitely a learning experience. Try on designs to make sure they work on human bodies. Anticipate and budget for problems. Produce shorter runs. After the

Nipplegate debacle, I stuck with runs of six shirts. Cheekys was so small, that was enough to stock the store and post a picture on Facebook. If a customer ordered one online, I'd yell to Justin, and he'd run to the shed and print it.

He still screwed up half the time.

Fortunately, I had a taker for those misprints: my best friend and silent business partner Trisha. She had married a hippie mountain man, retired across the border in rural Oregon, and gone granola. She liked to wander into the store unannounced and hang around for a few hours, harassing Morgan about her latest crush, entertaining my kids, and occasionally doing odd jobs, like shipping Facebook orders. The only payment she wanted was misprinted shirts. Every misprint cost us money in materials, of course, so if Justin botched a print job he used the shirt for practice. Trisha would take those shirts and walk down Plymouth Avenue with four designs—let's say kissing lips, an American flag, a belt buckle, and the word "Darlin'" in elaborate cursive—printed front, back, and over the shoulder.

"It's good advertising," she said.

"It's terrible advertising, Trisha. That shirt's a mess, and you look half homeless." I think she had stopped combing her hair.

Trisha laughed. "That's why people will remember."

There was no point in arguing. You gotta love your friends the way they are.

The second time I went to Dallas, I took my family. We take that trip twice a year now, and it is our big vacation. We stop at interesting sites along the way, like Native American reservations, historic battlegrounds, or national parks. By the time we hit

Texas, as Justin jokes, "There's a relative of Jessi's at every inter-state off ramp, or at least a Dairy Queen, which is almost as good."

My dad comes from a long line of West Texas plumbers. I have so many plumbers in the family, they must have laid pipe across the whole Permian Basin, the official name of the Texas oil region. I wasn't raised by that side of the family, but they are good, hardworking, mostly honest, redneck-as-all-get-out people. They took me in at eleven, and I can never repay them for the damage I brought with me. Over the years, we have visited so many aunts, uncles, and cousins I can't keep count, but starting that first year, we always made two stops: in Midland to see Granny Dee (until her death in 2016) and in Lubbock to pick up my dad.

When people think West Texas, they think Marlboro Man. Big. Masculine. Cowboy. Lung cancer. That's not my dad. I always wanted the Marlboro Man, but Pops (as everyone calls him) is no cattle puncher. He's about five foot six in both directions, up and around. He's been sporting a "skullet" for at least a decade, bald on top with a ponytail in the back. He's a sixth degree black belt in karate, but he spent his working life as an apartment complex maintenance man, something that embarrassed me as a teen, which was stupid, especially considering where I came from. It took becoming an adult to realize a maintenance man could be a great man: smart, kind, and loyal to the people he loved.

Pops didn't get to see much of my children. He was too West Texas. His tour of duty in the Air Force forced him to live in Germany and Missouri, and for dad, that only proved the old Texas adage that nobody should ever go north of Amarillo, especially after July. (It might snow.) That's why I treasured those twice-yearly visits. While Justin and I worked the Market, Pops took the kids to Legoland, the Aquarium, and other Dallas sites, like the knife show. Pops is a knife maker. He loves knife shows.

This second trip to Market, I wasn't just looking for merchandise. I placed a few orders, but mostly I studied designs. What worked? What didn't? I was creating my own shirts, and the best inspiration is something you love. One of my favorite brands, for instance, is Cowgirl Justice. They're a small company that does Western right. At their booth in Dallas, I noticed a "cattle brand" of their name on the bottom back of every shirt.

I thought it was tramp-stamp sexy, and who doesn't wanna feel sexy at a rodeo or bar? So I told Justin I wanted to put a belt-buckle-style Cheekys logo on the back of every shirt he printed.

"What? No…" he groaned. "That's another screen, Jessi. I'll have to turn each shirt over and print it an extra time. I thought we were going to make the process simpler."

Justin, who ever told you this was going to be simple?

That belt buckle—butt buckle?—was the first time the name "Cheekys" appeared on our merchandise, and our Facebook page blew up with women asking for more. Sure, the buckle was sexy, and it drew attention to the right place, but these women loved people knowing they wore Cheekys. They were upset whenever Justin accidently shortcutted a print run and forgot the stamp.

Wow, I thought. *They're proud to wear our clothes. They feel connected to us…*

We're a brand!

So many girls ask me, "When am I a brand?" Others think

they're one straight out of the gate. Personally, I don't feel you're a brand until people are asking for your name and paying money to wear it. Not everyone agrees with that, and I know you have to start somewhere, but work on your products, your image, and your marketing first. Understand what you're making and why. Have three failures, because they teach you what your customers want. Branding isn't a "fake it until ya make it" situation. It's "build it, sell it, then brand it...maybe they'll come."

The other important step forward in Dallas was tracking down the name I had heard over and over on my first visit to Market: Harry Hines. Harry Hines. Harry Hines.

Who in the heck, I had wondered, *is Harry Hines?*

I heard it the first time when I asked a woman at Market if she had an item in another color. Remember, I never settle for what's in front of me. I always ask if there's a better version. The woman said, "I don't have that here, but they might in our warehouse."

How disappointing. The woman was Chinese, so I assumed her warehouse was in Shanghai, or at least on the West Coast.

"It's only a couple miles away," she said.

Then she said that magic name: *Harry Hines.*

Back in Idaho, I noticed the return address on some of my Texas orders contained the same name: *Harry Hines.* So I went on Google and looked up the addresses. They were all within a few blocks of one another.

Turns out Harry Hines wasn't a person but a street. It was known for its glamorous shopping, but it also went through the Asian trading district—formerly (and inaccurately) known as China Town. So on my second trip to Dallas, I took my Google map and went looking for those addresses, with the family in tow. I don't like taking chances in strange neighborhoods. I wanted Justin there, just in case.

It didn't take long to realize Harry Hines was perfectly safe and full of bargains, if you knew where to look. Most of the largest wholesalers at Market were from Asia—not just China, but all over the eastern half of the continent. Right now, that's where the world manufactures. Many had warehouses in Harry Hines, where they sold the same products they showed at Market for half the price. That's a good tip if you're a store owner: shop around! Buying in Harry Hines as well as Market (you have to do both, because Market is so much bigger) can save a small boutique. But for me, finding mass-produced bargains wasn't enough. The real treasures were the small companies that created their own products. Finding them took persistence and a bit of luck.

For instance, I was in a massive warehouse in Harry Hines. This place had (no joke) three million fake flowers and ten thousand other things as well. It had a strict no-children policy, pretty fair given that twenty-foot-tall piles of random junk blocked every aisle, but that meant Justin had to wait outside with the kids.

When I came out, he was talking with an older Asian woman. Her English was good enough to understand and she was clearly fascinated with Jack and Sterling. She had spent most of her life in China under the one-child policy, where each family could have only one child, so she had very little experience with twins. She had one child, she told us. As it turned out, he manufactured belts.

Next thing I know, the woman is in the Yukalade directing us to her son's shop. It was way off the beaten track, down an alley, around multiple blind corners. There were graffiti, garbage, boxes piled by every door. Her son's door was the metal kind mafia goons kick open in the movies. It had no sign. But the man made amazing belts at fantastic prices.

Shopping from the source like that, you can personalize. You can choose the stones, the buckle style, the color, the thickness, the material. You're not "designing" belts. You are showing the belt guy the right combination of elements for your market. Many women get upset when they see their "designs" sold in other shops, but that's the business. Every time you "design" a piece from someone else's stock elements—meaning the stuff they have in their catalogues or ready-made for assembly—you are showing them what your audience wants, so they will turn around and sell that design to other vendors in your market. That's wholesale.

It's a practical issue, not greed. I could only afford to buy twenty of each belt I designed that day. But the belt man, who was small-batch manufacturing them, *not* making them by hand, needed to run ten dozen to make them affordable. (The more you manufacture, the cheaper each individual piece becomes; that's the concept underlying machine production.) What is he supposed to do with those extra hundred belts? He has to sell them, or our transaction doesn't work. The only way to avoid having him sell them to others is for me to buy all ten dozen. That's what the big guys do, and at that level, you can demand an exclusive. But Cheekys wasn't big enough to order like that until 2017. So I created the exact belts I wanted, down to the stamping, and contented myself knowing I had my personal perfect product, even if others might be selling them soon.

Then the belt guy directed me around the corner to some boot makers. They were Mexican, and Mexicans are incredible cowboys. Those cowboy boots are one of my best ever finds, because they *were* handmade. They were worth $500, but my customers couldn't afford that, so for two years I bought them for about fifty dollars and sold them for a hundred and a half.

The next day at Market, I made another small step forward— the kind that, when put together with the others, ultimately turns learning into earning. It was the last day of the show and, around closing, I noticed several vendors smashing their merchandise. These were ceramic lighthouses, animal sculptures, things I'd never sell at Cheekys, but still nice. Why would they do that? They had flown in from overseas, they explained, and it was cheaper to destroy the leftovers and file an insurance claim than to ship them back.

"Why don't you sell them to me?" I said.

I had no idea what to do with this stuff, since it didn't fit my brand, but at a dime apiece (or less) it was worth loading up the Yukalade and figuring it out later.

It was Trisha who suggested an auction, or maybe a yard sale... either way, an auction was the end result. I had a website, www.cheekysboutique.com, but it was just an ordering portal. I would post a photo on the Cheekys Facebook page, and if someone wrote back and said, "I love that, where can I order it?" I would go to the website, add that item, and Facebook her back with the link. "It's on our website. You can order it right here!"

Half the time, I was on my sofa in my pajamas, because I posted a lot at night. I would sit there, watching *Gold Rush* or *Parks and Rec* and refreshing the page, waiting for the order. When it came in, I'd yell, "I got one, Justin!" I thought I was so clever. Really, I was just small.

So that's how I started my auction business. I posted a notice on my Facebook page, then posted a couple items in a special section on my website. People were bidding within minutes. I posted a couple more items (while in my pajamas). More bids. So I posted all the items. Everything sold, some for more than I would have asked for if I was pricing it myself. Within a week, the auction brought in enough money to cover all my Dallas expenses.

And just like that, I was killing three birds with one stone...

No, Addy would strangle me if she heard I was killing birds. She loves animals, just like her dad. I was *freeing* three birds by opening one door. I was increasing the engagement with our customers and their connection with Cheekys; I was making money with very little upfront cost or risk; and I was giving Trisha something to do besides stroll around New Plymouth in ugly shirts, because I set up a separate auction website, www .cheekysauctions.com, and put her in charge. Trisha still runs our auction site, and it's a smashing success. It brings in thousands every week, but I pay her only $1,200 a month, because that's all she'll take.

That and a bunch of misprinted shirts.

When I opened a second Cheekys location in Nampa, a salesman from the local radio station suggested I advertise with them. It would cost $1,500, he told me, for ten spots. Only $150 per ad! Tempting, but...

I sat down and thought about what else I could do with $1,500, and here's what I came up with: I could hold a drawing and give away one pair of my exceptional quality boots every month for a year, and four pairs—a family pack!—in a grand prize drawing at Christmas. At a retail price of $150, that was $2,400 in giveaways, but since I purchased the boots for $50, it only cost me $800. And that cost wasn't right now, like the radio ads. I only had to find $50 a month and an extra $200 in December.

The boot promotion taught me a valuable lesson, because it brought in a ton of customers, and it made people happy—even the ones who didn't win liked checking in to see who had. So before you spend money on an ad, ask yourself: If I were to buy inventory and give it away, would it create more business? Would it create stronger relationships? What is my goal? Now, as a bigger brand, I do both ads and giveaways, but I still ask myself those questions and try to find the right balance, almost every day.

I loved those boots. They brought in good, steady money, and they brought in good customers, even after the giveaway ended. I thought I'd sell them forever. Then a small boutique in Nampa started selling them and undercutting my price. By a lot. So I went over and asked the owner about it. She said, "Oh, a friend found those boots for me when she was at Market in Dallas."

I knew her "friend" didn't find my boot guys on a trip to Dallas. Nobody could find that place. And from the look of her merchandise, this woman had never been to Harry Hines. But I remembered Granny Dee: *Be pretty, Jessi.* I let it go. (Kinda.)

A few weeks later, I discovered that someone had called the boot company and changed my address to hers. When the boxes arrived, the woman had just opened them up and started selling the boots. Scandalous, I know.

I still didn't confront her (too much). She had the contact for reorders, and she was selling dirt cheap. I didn't want her or her customers to think we were the same caliber of store, so I cleared out my stock and stopped selling the boots.

Customers still ask me, "What happened to your boots, Jessi? I loved those boots." Customers always seem to want what you no longer have.

I smile. "I decided to go a different direction. Have you seen our newest shirts?"

(continued)

The boots didn't matter. I mean, I needed the money. God, did I need it. But no one product will make or break a store. Period. Believe it. So you have to move on. Don't worry about the one you lost. Don't worry about *being right*. Worry about finding the next great thing. *Be Pretty.* You need all the allies you can get, in retail and in life.

And besides, that woman in Nampa—she probably had a family to feed, too.

CHAPTER 6

THE SECOND-YEAR WALL

And still, even with all that—the rodeos, the Facebook page, the tutus, the customer service, the pink barn, the auction, the shirt press, the hair salon, the original designs, the trips to Market and Harry Hines—Cheekys was only breaking even. That's the nature of the first phase of entrepreneurship, when you're struggling to carve out your space. Revenues rise, but not faster than the costs of more merchandise, more equipment, and more time on the road. Then little mistakes—from a couple hundred misprinted shirts to cell phone holders that become obsolete to a busted pipe in your hundred-year-old storefront (yes, it happened, and I paid to fix it)—eat up the rest.

It's the most dangerous time for a small entrepreneur, that space around two years, when you're exhausted and the excitement of your first successes is gone and you're tired of waking up early every day to *be pretty* to an angry new Facebook customer who didn't receive her order overnight like she does with Amazon.

"I've been at it a year," so many women post on the Hub. "I've been at it two years. I'm still broke. I don't think I can do it anymore."

Ask yourself: What else are you going to do? I'm serious. Is there something available to feed your family that you want to do more? If so, do that. Life is short. If not—if you really care about your business and feel it's an important part of who you are and who you want to be—push through. Keep innovating. Keep trying new things.

The wall is real. That feeling you're up against it, and you're never going to make it: it's real. I've been there a dozen times, with all the fears and anxieties, but walls are for climbing. You can get over it, whatever it is, if you commit to not only working hard but working smart. You can get over this wall and move on to the next.

It wasn't Cheekys crushing me against the wall in 2013, though. It was the custody battle for my twins.

A custody fight isn't like television. There's no high-stress courtroom testimony. There's no chance to dramatically profess that you will die for your boys and that nothing can overpower a mother's love. In fact, there's no courtroom or testimony. Mostly, it's filing documents back and forth. But I was floored by the documents Nick produced.

He went after everything I knew he would: our income, our debt, the fact Justin and I had both been married before, our rumored but completely untrue "drug habits" and "child abuse." He used Justin's depressive episode to argue he was mentally ill and should be kept away from children. He claimed we were unemployed, since we "only" ran a store.

I am always amused when people say stuff like, "Oh, you don't really have a job. You're self-employed." The truth is, you've never worked your butt off until you've put your life on the line for your dream.

It was the other stuff that floored me, though. Nick had videos of Justin and me. Many times, I had suspected I was being followed. Here was the proof. Nick had had private investigators tailing us since Texas. He had records, receipts, and investigative reports on totally ordinary things I'd done. He had Hunter and Addy's school records. He tried to use absences and detentions against us. Everything was exploited and manipulated, no matter how small.

He had screen grabs of my conversations with customers from the Cheekys Facebook page. We sold products with pictures of guns on them, such as a hat with crossed pistols. Does anybody really have a problem with that? Especially in rural Idaho. They said the guns showed we were violent and immoral.

As Justin and I said to each other dozens of times, "Don't these people have anything else to do with their time and money?"

The answer was clearly no...and that terrified me. All those videos. All those private investigators. It was suffocating. I felt naked and exposed. I was being watched, I was being filmed, and I was being judged. That's the main reason that, after my first trip to Dallas in 2012, I didn't post my face on the Cheekys Facebook page again until 2017. I've always had anxiety. I've always felt unworthy. It's one of my proudest accomplishments to overcome my fear and self-doubt to put myself out there to the world, even in this book—especially in this book—but Nick sent me crashing backward into anxiety. I never knew what totally innocent thing he was going to try to use against me.

Justin and I had already had our family observed twice, once by the county when the anonymous abuse accusations started, and once by the state after Nick sued for emergency custody. This was a multi-week process where experts watch you in your home, investigate your business, interview your children, check your financial records, etc. Justin and I passed both times. In fact, the two women who performed the state observation testified on our behalf at the custody hearing. They said Justin and I were loving parents.

The judge ordered a home study anyway. This was a three-month process where an evaluator would be with us periodically to observe our actions and interview the people around us. He was an older man. In fact, this was his last assignment before retiring. He had a quiet demeanor. It was almost like a joke: there was a man in our house with a clipboard taking notes, but he never talked to us about what he was writing. Talk about anxiety-inducing.

Since this book deal, I've had calls about being on a reality television show. Believe me, that is the last thing I want. I've been followed, filmed, observed, and judged. I hated it. Every minute that man was in our lives, I was thinking, *What am I doing? How will he see it? Is this something that, in some way, could cost me my sons?* And that was just while cooking dinner!

And oh yeah, it's not easy having a guy like that in your store. *What's he doing?* I imagined customers thinking when they glanced his way.

Oh, you know, just checking to see if I'm such a terrible mom the state needs to take my children away. So . . . do you like that purse?

I was honest with him about everything. Honesty is the best policy, right? I knew Nick would hammer me on my childhood, saying the way I was raised made me unfit to raise my own children, so I told the evaluator the truth, the whole truth, and nothing but the truth.

My mother was a fifteen-year-old runaway, although my dad didn't know she was so young. He was eighteen and in basic training. When mom got pregnant, she followed him to the air force base in Germany where he was stationed, but she was sent home after a violent incident with another woman. She raised me in a dilapidated strip mall across the street from the main entrance to Sheppard Air Force Base in Wichita Falls, Texas. It was a nasty property with nothing but a bar, a strip club, a porn shop, and a deserted storefront where the roof and front wall had collapsed years before. That collapsed storefront was my playground, while mom entertained clients at the strip club next door.

The strip mall was owned by W, the man I was forced to call "daddy." He was a black man in his mid-fifties (mom was a teenager back then, remember), and he was my mother's manager, boyfriend, employer, and abuser. For years, W moved mom and me between neglected properties he owned all over Wichita Falls and the surrounding area. Most had no electricity. Only a few had running water. I knew we were hiding, but I didn't know what from. It turned out in part to be my father, who had moved back to Texas and was looking for me.

I don't know why mom clung to me so hard. She was incapable of showing me any love, care, or concern. She was an addict, narcissist, and con woman. That's why other mothers pointed me out to their children and said, "Never talk to that little girl. She's a bad, bad child." It wasn't just the stripping, the drugs and addiction. Mom conned everyone who ever tried to help her. To touch her life in any way was to be used and discarded. Everyone assumed I was like her.

But there are three ways you can go in a situation like that: You can accept it and try to make the best of it, you can become broken from the pain and abuse, or you can run in the opposite direction. My younger sister, whom I helped birth on a dirty mattress in an abandoned house when I was eight years old, came closest to the first. She stayed close to mom, although she never went to such dark places in her own life. My youngest sister suffered the second. She was institutionalized by my mother as a teen, and she was heartbroken and sick with fear and disgust for years. She's awesome now. (She asked me to use that word, by the way.) We usually talk at least twice a week by phone, and she's one of my best friends. She managed to move on, finally, with the help of her wonderful husband and family.

I chose the last.

I mean, I tried like hell to please my mother. By six, I was bagging magazines in the porn shop and ironing money. By seven, I was cooking her breakfast on the rare mornings when she was awake and able to eat. Whenever the elementary school sponsored candy or catalogue sales contests, with prizes for selling the most, mom drove me to the far side of town first thing Saturday morning and dropped me off.

"When it gets dark tonight, baby," she said, "go into someone's house and use their phone to call me. I'll come pick you up."

I did it every time. I walked and sold candy and cookies and trinkets until my feet bled through my socks. Mom wanted that prize, and I got it for her, every time, because I wanted her love. I wanted her to think I mattered.

Of course those experiences scarred me. I know that, although it's been hard to admit. I was the top seller on the biggest used car lot in Boise for several years in a row, and the men hated me for it. They felt they had to put me in a woman's place, which to them meant underneath. They said things like, "If I had a body like you, I'd be the top seller, too."

It chilled me. I mean it, I got cold. I felt afraid, not necessarily of them, but because men had been commenting on my body like that for as long as I could remember, and I had no protection. None. The one time I confessed my fear of grown men's attentions to my mother, she snapped, "Oh, I assumed you lost your virginity a long time ago." I was eleven.

I wasn't afraid of work. Even at six, I could sell anything. But I would never, ever sell anything like that. God gave me a talent to hustle so I could survive, I always say, but he gave me a conscience so I could live. I wasn't like my mother.

I told you earlier I dropped out of high school and ran away from home two months before graduation. That's true, but it wasn't my mother's home. It was the state home for troubled girls, where I was committed at the age of fifteen. My father had rescued me when I was eleven. He took me into his home. But I couldn't live with him. I had no idea how to have a parent, much less one who loved me. I didn't even know how to be a child. So I ran away. Granny Dee and Daddy Joe took me in, and I ran away from them, too: I have no idea why. There are so many things in my childhood I don't remember, and so many other things I don't understand.

But this is the one thing I do know: None of that made me a bad mother to my own children. In fact, it made me a great mother, because nobody was more committed to loving and protecting her family than me. I would die for my children. Some of that, probably, is because my own mother never gave a shit about me.

I don't know if that evaluator listened. He wrote his notes, he nodded, but he never said anything about what I told him, not even "I'm sorry you had to go through that." On the day he left, Justin and I had no idea what his decision would be.

Two weeks later, we lost our house. Our lease-to-own deal was up, but we didn't have the savings or credit necessary to buy it. We had pushed our purchase date back twice already, and the owner wouldn't do it again. He sold the house to someone else.

Thankfully, we found another lease-to-own on the other side of New Plymouth. It's the 1902 farmhouse with four acres we live in today. We were lucky, because I like this house much better. It's smaller but cheaper, and our neighbor Dave raises corn and alfalfa instead of dairy cows, so the view and the smell are better.

The previous owners were an older couple, and the house wasn't in great shape. Justin started tinkering (tinkering to him is refinishing the floors) like he always does, and a few days after we moved in, Addy ran into our bedroom early on a Saturday morning. "Mom, dad, there's water running down the walls!"

"Who left the shower running?" Justin barked, thinking it had overflowed.

But it wasn't the shower. It was a busted pipe. Justin had to pull out twelve tons of lathe and plaster in the living room and bathroom, and since there was plumbing to be fixed, and a floor to be sanded and refinished, and we couldn't afford any of it, he nailed clear sheeting to the studs and stretched it around the room to cover the exposed insulation. It was like living in a plastic grocery bag.

So if you feel like giving up...if you feel like you can't do what I've done because you haven't made enough progress in your life already...remember me in that moment: beyond broke, more than overworked, emotionally exhausted, in a house with no interior walls, desperately trying to retain custody of my sons.

I remember thinking, *Thank God the home study evaluator can't see us now.*

Not long after, we received his report. It was twenty-eight pages long, and while it was a bloodbath back and forth—the man never heard a rumor, apparently, he didn't feel like writing down without comment or investigation—he seemed to recognize that Justin and I were good parents. I could feel the relief washing over me as I read it. It was like taking off layer after layer of heavy, sweat-drenched coats and finding the strength to slowly stand up straight again. It was over. I had passed all the tests. Sure, the report was ugly in spots, both ways, but it was clear this man knew I was a loving mom. I was going to keep primary custody of my sons.

Then, on the second to last page, he said the boys had a better relationship with Nick's extended family, because I came from a broken home. Then he called my financial situation unstable, noting that Nick had a newer house than me (even though Nick admitted earlier in the document the house was owned by his mom). He claimed—and this one hurt, because I had been a room mother at their school since the boys were in kindergarten—that Nick's attention to Jack and Sterling's education was better than mine and that, "While the evidence is not strong it does suggest…children tend to do somewhat better when living with parents of the same sex as the child."

It was a sledgehammer to my heart. It almost killed me. The twins had a dad in my home. They had a great dad. He had been there since they were two months old, and he had loved and cared for them every day. But Justin's love and commitment didn't count, according to this old man. And neither did mine, at least not as much, because I was only their mom.

I called my attorney. He said, "If you want to keep fighting, I need five thousand dollars by Friday."

I didn't have $5,000, but maybe I could borrow it...

"And another twenty thousand by the end of the month."

My heart sank. It was broken already. What else would it do?

"I can't get you that kind of money," I said.

"Then you better start negotiating."

I met with Nick and his lawyer for arbitration before the court ruling. I asked Nick to come out into the hall to talk privately, but he would only come as far as the door. I said, "Please Nick. Please don't take my sons. I will do anything. I will get on my knees and beg. I can't live without them."

"Good," he said. "You should get down on your knees and beg."

I lost residential custody of my boys. They were taken from me and placed primarily with Nick. I would have them only every other weekend during the school year, every other holiday, and half the summer.

It felt like they died. It felt like the best part of me died, too. I had been through so much growing up... I had fought so hard to bring Cheekys to the brink of success... but this broke my spirit. I lost my joy. I lost my ability to smile, even into the mirror when I was alone.

I went into mourning. I hit the wall and fell backward, into the deepest hole of my life. The only thing I remember thinking that wasn't dark, dark, dark was *I will die before I let this happen again. I will work myself to death. I will make Cheekys a success. I will never let anyone hurt my family, ever again, because I don't have the money to fight.*

That was hard. Hard for me, at least, because it hurt so bad. It hurts right now, writing these words, thinking about that old man's recommendations, remembering the feeling of losing my sons. But that's not the end of the story. In fact, we're only in the middle. So let's take a quick break and talk about something positive, like inner strength, marriage, and the rewards of persevering through un-positive things.

I got married at nineteen. Let's start there. I got pregnant at twenty-one. I spent those first two years selling Mary Kay. Businesses like Mary Kay are a lifeline to mothers. They allow us to make extra money while staying home and setting our own hours. I can't begin to guess how many hardworking families have been saved by Mary Kay. It must be a million. I love Mary Kay for that.

Then Ben and I moved from Texas to his hometown of Elk City, Oklahoma, a dot on the map, at least back then. I only knew seven women in Elk City, all through Ben, and four of them sold Mary Kay. Without my business, I felt lost. I didn't need money. Ben had moved home for a good job in the oil field, but Elk City wasn't my home, and I hated having no identity other than as Ben's wife.

Then Ben cheated on me. Not a one-night stand, either. A side piece. Hunter was only a couple months old when I found out, so I was already exhausted and emotional. I cried for days. I punished myself for what I'd done wrong. I'd gained more than fifty pounds during the pregnancy that I couldn't lose. I'd been sick and needy. It had to be that, right? It had to be me. That's what cheaters do. They make you doubt yourself.

Finally, I sat down and looked at myself in the mirror. I said: "Jessi, you are twenty-one years old, and you are unhappy, overweight, unemployed, and married to a man who doesn't respect you enough not to screw other women, even though you just gave birth to his child. How did this happen?"

I struggled as a teen. I was a mess. Nobody treated me well, especially boys, who assumed I was easy. I wanted to blame that on my mother, but Daddy Joe wouldn't hear it. Whenever I bitched about being picked on or used, he said, "Is that a door, Jessica Dawn, or is that a mirror?"

He meant the lack of respect wasn't coming from outside; it was a reflection of my actions and thinking. If I didn't like myself, and I didn't stand up for myself, then that's the way others would treat me.

(continued)

I was scared when Ben cheated on me. I didn't know who I was without him or if I could make it on my own. And I was prideful. I didn't want to admit I had failed at my marriage. But I had to respect myself, because no one was going to do it for me. So I left Ben. I took my baby, moved to a tiny one-bedroom apartment in Midland, Texas, and got a job waiting tables at the Outback Steakhouse. A younger friend called during my week of waitress training. She was in Houston; her boyfriend was mixed up in drugs; she was broke, homeless, and terrified.

I said, "If I buy you a ticket, will you get on the next bus to Midland?"

"Yes."

"Don't lie to me, Ivy. Please. This is my last sixty bucks, and I need it bad."

She showed up the next morning on the overnight bus. I said, "You can live with us for as long as you want, rent free, but you're Hunter's babysitter now."

My first week with my own tables, I had a family of four where everything that could go wrong went wrong. It was an hour of hot white wine, cold food, wrong orders, long delays, and screaming kids. As he was handing me the check, the father said, "Is this your career, young lady, or are you just doing it to get by?"

I was ashamed. I said, "I'm sorry, sir. That meal was not as it should have been. If you give us another chance I will learn from this and make sure it's better next time."

He put up his hand to stop me. "Have you ever considered selling cars?"

"Um...no, sir."

"My name is Chris Robin," he said. "I run a Saturn dealership. If you're interested in a career in cars, come see me."

I was like, *Are you kidding? After the worst meal of your life?*

I asked Chris later, after he became my mentor and friend, what he saw in me that night. He said I took responsibility, communicated, and refused to blame others. "You owned that situation," he said. "You handled it like I would have wanted my employees to handle it."

I still didn't know about the job. I almost turned it down. It was on commission, so there was no guaranteed money. I had a baby and Ivy to take care of, and I didn't know a thing about cars.

"How much you making at Outback?" Chris asked.

"Sixteen hundred dollars a month." That was a lie. It was less than a thousand.

"What if I guarantee you sixteen hundred the first month, no matter how many cars you sell?"

"I don't know," I said. "That's so short-term. I can't afford to be out of work come October." Not to mention, I was interviewing in a construction trailer on a dirt lot. This guy might be out of work by October for all I knew.

(continued)

"What if I guarantee you thirty-two hundred for the first month?" Chris said. "If ya don't make it, you'll have cushion to go find that dream waitress job of yours." He kinda snickered.

"What's so funny?" I asked. Looking back, I can't believe that came out of my mouth. It seemed like a scam, and I was the scammer. There was no way I was good enough for this job or that much pay.

"Oh," Chris said, "I am just looking forward to reminding you a year from now, when you ask for a raise, that sixteen hundred dollars a month is all you really need."

I took the job. I worked six days a week, ten hours a day, while Ivy stayed in my apartment with Hunter. At the end of the first month, Chris called me into his office. "I'm giving you the afternoon off," he said. *Oh, God, I'm fired.*

He gave me my check. It was almost $3,500, because my sales commissions were more than my guarantee. "Now go get some decent dress clothes, J. D. I'll see ya tomorrow."

You know those movie scenes where the woman is in the middle of the store with a shopping bag in each hand spinning around and around with a giant smile on her face? Well, that was me in Mervyn's. I felt like I could buy the world. I bought four outfits for work, basically the same outfit in four different colors. I bought clothes for Hunter. I bought an outfit for Ivy. I bought boots and three pairs of shoes. And deodorant and diapers, the fancy ones that changed colors when they're wet. We went to Outback Steakhouse that night and ate like we'd won the lottery. The next morning, I was on the lot selling Saturns at nine a.m.

Ivy lived with us for six months. We only had one bed, so we slept in shifts, but those were some of the best months of my life. We laughed and played hip-hop and seventies soul, and Hunter took his first steps and said his first word, "saur-saur." (I'm pretty sure it meant dinosaur.) I was a mom. I was a success. Our happiness was a mirror. I never could have given Hunter that if I had stayed with Ben.

It doesn't always work out that way. I'm not saying it does. Up until losing my twins, Ben cheating was the worst moment of my adult life. It was worse than Nick walking out when I was pregnant, because I loved Ben.

But you're powerful, girl. You can beat this, whatever it is. You can overcome anything. You just have to take control. You have to listen to the people who say you can, instead of the people who say you can't. You have to be that positive person for yourself. You have to look in the mirror and say, "This is my only life. I'm gonna live it my way."

I still see Ben from time to time. We regularly text and talk on the phone. We raised Hunter together, even though Ben lived a thousand miles away, and we're better friends than ever. We even got back together for a while, until Ben cheated again.

(continued)

When I told him about this book, Ben said, "Aw, shit, Jess, I'm going to look like a real asshole."

I laughed because, well, yeah, Ben, you treated me wrong.

But Ben's not an asshole. He's a good man, just a lousy husband, at least when he was young. He's one of my biggest supporters. We grew into adults together; we loved and lost people together; and, most important, he is the best father to Hunter he knows how to be. When Hunter showed his pig at 4H, Ben not only flew up from Texas to watch, he bought the pig at auction. Paid way over top dollar, too—which might have been because Justin convinced a friend to bid up that wealthy out-of-town oil driller.

Leaving Ben was hard. It was so, so hard. But it changed my life. It allowed me to prove myself *to myself* and become the Boss Lady I am today. It gave me a confident kid, a great second husband, and the perfect ex—a supportive friend who will always be there for me and our son . . . and doesn't mind, every now and then, if he's being had.

CHAPTER 7

CHEEKYS CHICKS

I started the Cheekys Chicks in the spring, a few months before the home evaluator took a sledgehammer to my family's life. My Nampa store was up and running, but it wasn't generating the extra revenue I needed for the custody battle, so I had to buckle up my big-girl pants, get out in my community, and find more customers.

That was hard for me. I'm not social, in the conventional sense. I don't go to bars. I don't go out to eat. I never went to parties, and I never got invited, anyway. I wasn't asked to be on committees or welcomed into the mom section at Hunter's football games. I was great in the store. I loved that one-on-one interaction, and my customers loved me back. They said to Morgan, "Oh, I know the owner." Or: "I'm a friend of Jessi's."

Morgan always laughed, as she told me many times, because Morgan is mouthy, whenever a customer said that: *Well, that's weird*, she thought, *because Jessi only has one friend, and you're not Trisha.*

Honestly, my confidence was shot. I felt like everyone was looking down on me because of the rumors, because I was being sued for custody, because I was in danger of losing my kids. I'd go to the grocery store and convince myself there was hate in strangers' eyes: *What kind of mother,* I'd image them thinking, *loses her children? What is really going on in that house?*

I needed help, in both my business and my life. So I put out a call out on Facebook: *Looking for young women to be Cheekys brand ambassadors at rodeos, stock shows, concerts, and parades in exchange for free merchandise.* As a marketing idea, it was right on brand. It was cheap, local, and targeted at my core audience.

I included a long application form, of course. I'm talking about a form that literally asked questions like "Can you drive a tractor?"

We're rural. We know farm equipment. A true Cheekys Chick, especially then, was an ag girl. And if she knew her way around a tractor, that meant someone in her family had enough money to own a tractor, which meant they were a pretty big deal.

After a few months, I invited the fourteen semifinalists to the store for an interview. I didn't tell anyone, but they were the only fourteen who applied. That isn't to say they were the only people interested, because another girl showed up.

"I think I'm supposed to be here," she said.

She was a rodeo queen, which isn't a metaphor. Each rodeo has a queen, so there were dozens of queens in southwest Idaho. It was like a club. The queens served for a year, so they tended to travel together and see each other at events. They even had a look. I knew a brown-haired girl who won rodeo queen because she was the best barrel rider in the northwestern United States, but by the time she took her throne she had blond hair half a foot high. I'm not opposed to that. As one of our shirts says, "The higher the hair, the closer to God." But that pressure—of being blond and beautiful and *on*—really messed with that girl. She was a smart, talented rider, but it took her three years to realize she could be herself without letting anyone down.

It's not the title that made you who you are, girl, it's who you are that got you the title. I hope that's something every queen knows, because it's an honor that can make even the best of them doubt their worth.

The girl who showed up at Cheekys probably felt that pressure, I don't know. What she came across as, though, was entitled. She was one of the prettier and more popular girls in the area. She felt that *of course* I was going to take her, because a girl like that can really help a little shop like Cheekys.

But her application was late and incomplete. So I turned her away. I have nothing against rodeo queens. I love rodeo queens. We women need to stick together: no pettiness or jealousy. It's not easy to be a pretty girl, when that's all anyone wants to see. I knew she was a good kid. But I needed girls who were willing to work.

I remember standing in my tiny store, looking at those young women. Fourteen, and the space was overflowing! There was Morgan, barely seventeen. Miranda, another local high school girl, had come into Cheekys a few months before with an incredible purse. I tried for months to track it down, but it turned out it was hand-painted by her Native American aunt, so I invited

Miranda to apply for the Chicks instead. Promise, Cheekys' primary hair stylist, was the closest thing I had to a second friend. She had big hair, big makeup, and a big personality. We dieted together, laughed together, hung out at my house with our kids, grilling and making cookies. We were in Ontario, Oregon, in the middle of a diet one year, waiting for a kids' clothing store to open for Black Friday, and there was a danged Carl's Junior right in our line of sight. After about an hour of staring at it, Promise said, "Why don't we buy a grilled beef burrito, chew up a bite and spit it out, just so we can taste it?"

"Girlfriend," I said, "I was thinking the same thing." We didn't do it, but that's how compatible we were.

I didn't know the other girls as well, but they were from all over the Payette Valley: Boise suburbs like Caldwell, little towns like Nyssa, and ranches in the high plains. They were country girls, dressed in their best boots and tees, their tight jeans and button-ups. They were short, round, tall, thin, and everything in between, but mostly they were young, in their late teens or early twenties. They were so nervous, they weren't even talking to each other. They weren't sure what was going on. And neither was I.

I thought, *You can't just use these girls for marketing, Jessi. You have to mentor them. Making them Cheekys Chicks means trying to make them better women, too.*

I didn't cut any of the semifinalists, as I had planned. Instead, I pampered them. I let them choose their favorite Cheekys clothes and accessories; Promise did their hair and makeup; and a local photographer took their pictures. We don't baby our daughters in the country. We expect them to rope, ride, and haul. I've had five grand champion ribbon holders in the Chicks, and others who became pro-level barrel racers and nationally recognized FFA (Future Farmers of America) officers. But every one of those tough country girls teared up when they saw their photos. They had always thought of themselves as *good* and *useful,* but they had never seen themselves as beautiful.

I knew that feeling. As a child, no one ever showed me how wonderful I could be, just by being myself. If someone called me beautiful, I was terrified of what they wanted from me.

After the photo shoot, I met with the girls and talked about our brand. I wanted these chicks to understand and reflect what Cheekys stood for: good merchandise at a great price, but also friendliness, kindness, respect for others, and a country lifestyle. We talked about manners. We talked about boys. We talked about how to answer questions and get people to open up. I wanted them approachable, not on a pedestal like the queens. Never look down on anyone, I told them. I didn't care if they had their hair done or their makeup on, every Chick had to *Be Pretty* when she represented the brand. That wasn't about looks. It was about the confidence to be kind.

Many of these young women were like me. They were good in their world, but out in public, they were introverted and unsure. But I saw them grow. I saw them smile when little girls asked for autographs and told them, "I want to be like you when I grow up." Yes, part of that was because they were running flags at the rodeo opening ceremony and wearing glittering rhinestone belts. Every little girl loves rhinestones. But mostly, it was because the Chicks were comfortable, confident, and having fun—especially when ten or twelve of us got together at a big event. That was a blast.

I don't want this to sound too altruistic. I was using those girls, too. That was a lonely year, and I needed allies. I needed respected girls from respected families to say good things about me when people claimed I was a drug addict and a child abuser. I needed to walk into a room with strong women by my side, because my heart was shattered, and I didn't have the courage at that moment to do it on my own.

It wasn't easy for them. Miranda dated a boy who had grown up with Nick. His family went to events and barbeques with Nick's family. After I hired Miranda as my second employee, her boyfriend's grandmother objected. "That woman is a terrible, trashy person," she said. "I hear all the time she is so much drama."

Miranda didn't back down. She said, "Well, I know Jessi, and respectfully, she's not like that at all." She did that half a dozen times with that family, and I will always love her for that.

Last year, Miranda married an airman. When she heard they were being stationed at Sheppard Air Force Base in Wichita Falls, she told me, "I know you had bad experiences there. I am so glad I can give that town new meaning for you. Jessi, I will make the best new memories for you there."

Having good people like that on my side. Having my Chicks speak up for me not out of duty but because they knew me, and they knew I was a good person...

It's a gift. It's what makes life special. It was something I needed, desperately, because saying I was depressed after losing custody of the twins is an understatement. I cried myself to sleep every night, if I slept. I dragged myself through every day. After the judgment, Nick tried to have my name removed from the twins' documentation, like their school registration and doctor records. He tried to have me barred from their Little League baseball games and their elementary school, where I had been a volunteer room mother for years. I had to constantly fight for my rights. I had to explain over and over again to egotistical men and judgmental women that, yes, I had lost residential custody, but I was still Jack and Sterling's mom.

The Chicks helped me through that. When we walked into an event together, I didn't feel alone. I didn't feel like a pariah. I felt like people looked at me as a resource for the community, not a child-loser. The Chicks didn't know they were doing that for me. They were just being themselves.

The biggest event around here is the Snake River Stampede. It's a major stop on the rodeo circuit, with five days of championship-level competition. One of the early, midweek nights was called Pink on the Dirt, and it was dedicated to breast cancer awareness.

I wanted Cheekys to be a part of it. This was right after I lost the twins, so maybe this was about proving I wasn't a loser, I don't know, but I wanted to help. Unfortunately, sponsorships started at $15,000—about $14,900 more than I could afford. So I found a smaller opportunity. Each year, Pink on the Dirt selected forty local women, mostly breast cancer survivors, but also a few local bigwigs and hospital executives, for a fashion show. They were given clothes and accessories by a sponsor, then "modeled" them at a fund-raiser in the middle of the massive dirt arena before the rodeo.

These women are brave, I thought. *They aren't standing in front of a crowd just for women with breast cancer. They are standing up for me, and every other woman, too.*

It was an honor for Cheekys to be chosen for the fashion show. It was a struggle to afford it, especially after my custody-related legal bills, but nothing close to the everyday struggle of these women for their health. We requested all of the breast cancer survivors, because those women were like us: they were fighters, they were from the country, and they were in need of feeling beautiful. The fashion show was one of the very few non-Sundays I closed Cheekys, because I took my whole staff and all of the Chicks with me. We stuffed the Yukalade with clothes, so each woman would have real choices. Sponsors like Cabela's took back their clothes at the end of the night. I planned to give each woman the outfit she wore, so she didn't feel like this was one-night-only, but a way she could live.

Our models were nervous. Most were in treatment, so they didn't feel like themselves. They had gained or lost weight; they were pale from radiation; they'd had breasts removed. It's tough to go in front of a crowd like that, especially when treatments sap your energy. And these were ordinary women. They were old, young, big, small, and unique like the rest of us. How many of us would feel comfortable modeling clothes in front of our neighbors? Not me. How much harder would it be if we were sick and there were hundreds of people watching?

One woman had been wearing a wig since chemotherapy. She hadn't gone out in public for six months without her hair on, but she took the wig off to try on outfits, and she was shocked by what she saw in the mirror. It was her true self, and she was lovely. She wanted to model like that, but it was a big step, so a few Chicks talked her through her feelings. I loved that about my Chicks; they cared about other women. In the end, the woman sat alone for a while, looking at her Cheekys outfit and her bald head.

"This is the best I've felt about myself in a long time," she said. Then she went in front of the crowd and showed them what true beauty looks like.

I thought, *This is it, Jessi. This is Cheekys. This is not just my purpose, it's my brand.*

That experience changed me. It showed me the kind of company Cheekys could be. After Pink on the Dirt, I shifted the Chicks to focus more on charity events, especially those for women and girls. I don't think a store can survive without supporting local causes. Giving isn't about customer relations; it's about remembering who you are and why you're here. If you only give when it's easy, you aren't giving at all. That's in the Bible.

A few months later, I started the Mother Hens for older women. Soon after, I created the Chicklets for girls in grade school. I didn't ask them to, but the Chicks took the little ones under their wings. They supported them at sporting events and when they showed stock. Do you know how much it means to a twelve-year-old girl to have ten cool women in their late teens and twenties cheering her on? It means the world, especially to the girls who don't have much support at home.

Do you remember earlier, when I said Cheekys was about helping country women find a community, see the beauty inside, and learn the value of who they are? You probably thought, *Jessi's crazy. She sells jewelry and shirts!*

Well, this is what I was talking about. Being Cheekys Chicks empowered those girls by showing them the beauty of their true selves. In return, they empowered me, because that's when I started to realize Cheekys wasn't my company. It was for all the women who found validation and recognition in our brand. With the right community, messages, and products, I realized, Cheekys could give them the confidence to become what I wanted every woman to be: sassy, country, ornery, and kind.

The fall after I started the Chicks, I served as a room mom
in the twins' third grade class. Their teacher, Shannon, was
surprisingly standoffish. Usually when people were like that, it
meant they'd heard about me through Nick, but in this case,
Nick had gone out of his way to tell me he didn't like her. So
I decided to not worry and *Be Pretty*. I ate lunch with her. I
offered as much help as I could. This was about being there
for and with the boys. Because of the custody ruling, it was
almost my only time with them during the school year.

Then one day at lunch, Shannon said, "Can I ask you a
question? It's kind of out there, but can you be honest with me?"

"Sure."

"I heard you don't like me," she said, and she started
crying. "I heard you said I couldn't be a good teacher because
I can't have children of my own."

My jaw dropped and my heart sunk. I was devastated
by the cruelty. Shannon had recently had a miscarriage,
and afterward she found out she couldn't have children.

(continued)

Who would use that against her? Who would speak such awful words to her, even when trying to put those words in someone else's mouth?

"It's not true," I said. "I would never say or think something like that."

"It bothered me so much," she said, wiping her tears. "It broke my heart. But you were so nice. You didn't seem like the type of person who would judge me that way."

I thought it must have been Justin's mom. She was a room mother, too; I figured it would take a woman to be so cruel. We have a terrible habit of trying to destroy each other.

I found out later it was Nick. He admitted to it in a deposition. Certain types of men, I've learned, are always trying to turn us women against each other.

But Nick didn't realize that when women are kind and honest with each other, we can break that cycle. Instead of judging each other, we can stand together. That's what happened with Shannon and me. Nick didn't build a wall; he created a bond. Shannon was my cheer coach leader for four years and a good friend. She's a positive, amazing role model for my family, including Addy, who had her as a teacher two years later.

I formed a similar bond with Mandy, one of our Mother Hens. During the week, Mandy was power suits and professionalism, but on the weekend she was dirty cowgirl boots, cut-off shorts, and mud drags with a longneck in her hand. She was business in the front, redneck in the back, and I loved her for it. So when I heard her daughter had been kicked in the head by a horse, I immediately called the Chicks.

You know what? They had already heard and were organizing on their own. Before the Chicks, those girls would have thought, *Why would she want to see me? What good can I do? I'll just be in the way.* There was a time I would have thought that, too. But now we knew we had value. We knew *sisterhood* had value, so the Chicks rushed to Mandy's side, and we stayed with her through the long weeks as the doctors worked to save Ariona's life.

Ariona not only survived, she made a full recovery. She became a well-known rider, a vocal proponent of horse safety (she barrel races in a helmet), and, two years after the accident, a Cheekys Chick, because she had seen the value in sisterhood, too.

Even better, in 2018, after five years of trying, I hired Mandy as Cheekys' human resources manager. I couldn't pay her what she was offered elsewhere, but she wanted to work for Cheekys, she said, "because this place makes me happy."

That's how good it can be, y'all, when we stand together. We can create happiness for ourselves and our sisters. We can build long-term, supportive, non-judgmental female relationships. And we can teach our daughters what it really means to *Be Pretty, Be Loyal,* and *Be Strong.*

CHAPTER 8

EXPANSION

DUMB AND SMARTER

My store in Nampa didn't work. That's why I haven't said much about it until now. Looking back, there are a number of obvious reasons for that:

1. It was in a suburban mall. Cheekys was a destination store, in an old-fashioned downtown. The location fit the style. A mall? Not so much.
2. It wasn't even a nice mall. The foot traffic was sparse, it was run-down, and I had overlooked some basic issues. If only one employee was working, for instance, she had to lock the store before going to the bathroom down a separate hall. Not a good idea.
3. It was more expensive than New Plymouth. That's the problem with the city.
4. Nampa was a growing suburb with shiny new big box stores. With so much cheaper competition, it was hard

to get customers who didn't already know Cheekys in the door—and I mean the door of that crappy mall, not just the store.

The real problem was more basic, though: I didn't need another store. The appeal of Cheekys was never its convenience. That's Walmart. Cheekys was about the experience. Women liked to come in and get their hair done. They liked to browse and talk with Morgan, Miranda, and me. Sure, I had a lot of customers from New Plymouth who liked having me five blocks away (everything in New Plymouth is five blocks away). Convenience mattered, but it wasn't a primary factor. There were women in Fruitland who thought New Plymouth was too far away to bother with, and that was a ten-minute drive. With the traffic in Boise, it could take an hour to get from downtown to the Nampa store. I could drive to Weiser faster, and Weiser is four towns away. In other words, our New Plymouth location wasn't a problem. It was an asset. It helped define what Cheekys was: a store for women in *this* town, and every town like it.

So I closed the Nampa shop. I wasn't losing money, but I was spending a lot of time and effort breaking even. I took that "free" time and moved the original Cheekys to a new location...directly across the street from the first store.

This had something to do with my landlord, who owned Truckstop.com. While most residents of New Plymouth wanted to keep the town as it was, Moscript the Younger—his father owned a large farm in the valley—was intent on changing it. He had leveled a block of our three-block downtown to build his super-tan stucco headquarters, which was fine, since that block was primarily a gas station and tire store. Then he bought every house on the downtown side of Holly Avenue and demolished them for his parking lot.

Most citizens were supportive. Scott Moscript grew up in New Plymouth, he was prominent in the local Mormon church, and his company provided more than a hundred good jobs. I wish he'd built an office building more in keeping with the area—it looks like it belongs in a Florida retirement community to me—but I guess some people don't like traditional Western, small-town architecture.

His headquarters was controversial, though, in one serious way: as the only three-story building in town, it was too tall for our fire department's equipment. They needed a new ladder truck to reach the top floor, but the town couldn't really afford it. Numerous plans were floated over the next six months, and I'm not sure what the solution was, but the department never got the new truck. Progress ain't easy, right?

Meanwhile, Moscript had been buying up the old 1920s storefronts on the west side of Plymouth Avenue. He owned all five between the Double Diamond and The Club, including the Cheekys location. Rumor had it his goal was to tear them down and build an indoor walking track. (It gets cold in Idaho in the winter.) If he'd gotten his hands on the Double Diamond when it was for sale in 2010, he might have done it. But neither Robin from the Double Diamond nor Heidi from The Club will ever sell to him. So he kind of lost interest in the properties—the four besides Cheekys were empty—and I was tired of Justin making all the repairs. We put thousands into that building just to keep it safe. And besides, we'd been growing for years. We needed a bigger space.

So we moved across the street to a redbrick building owned by the White family, who were original settlers of New Plymouth. Kerry White and her husband gave us a good deal: $450 a month for three times my original space, plus an attic and a basement and a big front window right next to the busiest spot in town—the Zion Bank ATM.

Getting the new Cheekys up and running was a challenge. The White building wasn't any more modern than Scott Moscript's space, so Justin updated the electrical, air conditioning, venting, and plumbing. In addition to working at Cheekys and as a volunteer fireman, I should probably mention that Justin is one of our fire code inspectors, so he followed rules to the letter—and loved it. As Hunter once said, half with exasperation and half with pride, "Dad doesn't care about money. All he cares about is building things."

Of course, when you have a husband like that, you save a lot of money. We spent a few hundred dollars on work that would have cost thousands. Sure, we set off the alarm at the Zion Bank half a dozen times, because the vault was set to detect vibrations in our shared wall. Sure, the sheriff was *annoyed*. But even with those delays, it was less than a month of twelve-hour days before Justin was pulling down another barn to decorate the store.

You may notice that's three barns demolished already, if you include the one I used for Nampa. Does that seem like a lot? Well, this is the country! Our new house was a former working farm, just like our first one, so our four acres were full of old cattle pens, haylofts, plow sheds, and covered corrals to protect livestock and horses against the hard Idaho winters. We've now pulled down five barns, and we still have one more tilting unused behind the house. And besides, we were able to reuse much of what Justin had built for the original store.

It was a group effort. Everybody pitched in. Morgan and Miranda—M & M, as I call them—hauled material and merchandise. Promise helped design and install the salon. Me, Trisha, and a rotating cast of volunteer Chicks painted. Hunter was down on his knees every weekend and after school, scraping off old lacquer and finish. I think we had to strip eight layers to get down to the original hardwood floors. Then everyone, including my ex Ben, who came up from Texas, helped refinish and stain them. The Double Diamond didn't open until ten—Robin keeps it open until at least midnight every day, even major holidays like Christmas, for people without a place to go—so Ken came over and worked with us every morning.

Ken was a fixture at the Double Diamond. As Robin says, she inherited him with the building. He had his own seat at the bar—second from the end, nearest the door—and if you needed a hand, that's where you'd find it. "For a couple beers Ken can do just about anything," Robin said once, "but you have to catch him early."

Ken died last year. He had a heart attack while helping a friend stack firewood for the winter. I don't go to the Double Diamond much, maybe twice a year. When you have a business and four children, you don't have the time or energy (or money) for bars. But every time I walk into the place, I touch the back of his chair and think of Ken. Not just because he was a good man, but because people like Ken make towns like New Plymouth special.

We opened "New Cheekys" in April 2014, and it was beautiful. Justin built shallow wooden corrals along the walls, so I could get creative with merchandise displays. The fourteen-foot ceiling was painted to look like stamped tin tiles. Justin replaced the fluorescent lighting with bare bulbs inside upside-down metal wash bins to make country chandeliers, and although those lights never quite shone as brightly as I would have liked, they were gorgeous. He built a full-size silo for the dressing room and hung my flying pig chandelier inside. And right in the center of the store, tying everything together, was a four-sided retail counter built like a barn, with beam supports and a shingle roof. Standing there, I was the queen of my kingdom, and my little kingdom was everything I had dreamed it would be.

Just as important, though, was the ugly space in the back, because it was my first real storage area and shipping center. Before, we were shipping out of the closet where I used to yell at Justin—and where the kids did their homework, I ordered my stock, and we ate so many family meals.

Gosh, that little closet was a big part of our lives.

But it was way too small for my shipping needs. When I started focusing on Internet sales in 2013, my goal was $200 in online orders a day—ten items at my average price. I rarely made my number, but that's how goals work, right? They make you stretch. Even when I moved into my new store, my monthly

Internet sales were only about $3,000, half of what I wanted them to be. But growing. Slowly.

My auction business, though, was huge. It was selling 200 items a week!

We had gone far beyond selling what I could buy for pennies at Market. Trisha and I were actively hunting for items at festivals, yard sales, and anywhere else the cool and unusual could be found. And the Chicks loved it. The auctions were sticky, as the business types say. They kept fans on our site for hours. It was like a game for them—the bidding, the commenting back and forth, the trash talking. I kept their credit card numbers on file so they could charge to their account, and I had more than a thousand. The info wasn't even electronic. It was index cards in a box.

That is not a good system, but I have a terrible habit of doing things old school. I mean, for the first year and half, I didn't even have a cash register. I wrote every transaction down in a spiral notebook and handwrote receipts. I know, crazy. So taking credit cards online was pushing it for me.

Then I signed up for PayPal. I cannot recommend PayPal highly enough. You pay them a portion of sales, but in return, they guarantee all payments. That's important. I know companies that were crippled or even bankrupted by credit card fraud.

I still accept credit cards, especially from the early fans. Those women are my core supporters, so I'll ride with their plastic 'til I die. But if I could convince every Chick to switch to PayPal I would, because it makes my life easier and my system less risky. So make a move. Try something new, not just with credit processing, but with everything. Life is about evolving. Never be scared of small changes.

PayPal allowed me to triple my order processing without worrying about scaling up my operations, but that left me with a shipping issue. I had a new space, but I had no shipping staff. No schedules or policies. No inventory tracking system, computer or otherwise. We all have our strengths. Shipping is not mine. I hate shipping. And shipping hates me.

So when I closed the Nampa store, I brought the store manager to New Plymouth to run my shipping operation. She was a short-term manager (less than a year) but a long-term customer, and I loved her. She was short and round with terrible teeth, but she was so friendly. She made everyone who walked in the door feel special, and that's exactly what I wanted. Hiring the prettiest girl is not always the best choice. I wanted people to know they didn't have to be pretty or perfect to wear our brand, and this woman was far from perfect. Like a lot of people around here, she had fallen into a meth habit as a young woman, but had a son, got married, and straightened herself out. When I hired her, she was sixteen years clean.

We were too small for a full-time shipping manager, so she split her time between the front of the store and the back. When they weren't busy, Morgan and Miranda pulled items for orders. When he wasn't on press or running errands, Justin packed. He and I spent many weekends in that back room, checking my printed page (so last century!) of weekly orders to make sure they had all gone out—which they never had, so we packed the leftovers ourselves.

I'm a stickler for the details, so I had specific rules for Cheekys boxes, labels, and packing paper. Everything a customer sees reflects your business, so make it right. I wanted opening our boxes to be a source of joy in their day, just like our online experience. That shouldn't have been hard. I mean, we only had three box sizes. Choosing the right one and keeping the packing paper neat was pretty much all you had to do.

And we still messed up constantly!

It didn't help that while the Cheekys merchandise was all roughly the same size, the stuff sold at auction was completely random. It might fit in our regular packages, or it might be a three-foot-tall ceramic giraffe. I didn't care as much about the look of the package, since the auction was not part of the Cheekys brand, but I couldn't afford broken necks.

The reality is, even when everything fits, shipping is hard. Big companies like Amazon have perfected a system by investing millions in computers and software and...I don't know... conveyor belts and "smart buildings" and surveillance. We're always going to be human beings at Cheekys, pulling each item from the shelf and putting it in a box by hand. Which might mean 200 mugs get broken because a shipper had a bad day and packed them wrong, and we have to make it right.

Fortunately, my customers have always been awesome. They have put up with our slow shipping times and mistakes. Even when we got backed up for weeks (it's happened once or twice), they stuck with us.

That's because we had a relationship. We were honest and

up-front and above all *human*, never hiding behind a logo. Customers knew us from the store or, since by then most lived outside Idaho, the Facebook page. That's where the real community lived, on Facebook. That's where Chicks complimented our posts and pictures. They posted messages and started discussions about favorite products. They even shared their own photos. That's the thing about the Facebook page. It started as a way for me to communicate with customers; it became a way for customers to communicate with me; it found its true purpose as a place where Chicks could communicate with each other.

But we were part of that conversation, always. You don't deserve new customers, after all, until you take care of the ones you have. My goal was for Cheekys to respond to every post within fifteen minutes, but it wasn't always possible. I had to sleep. I had to spend time with my children. I had to watch *Fixer Upper* and *Australian Border Patrol*. But I kept my phone close, so I could read and respond, even if the Australian Border Patrol had found the ingredients to make amphetamines in someone's luggage (again).

And if a Chick posted a problem? *That's fine.* I want to know so I can address it. I don't want to be insulted, but if an item wasn't the same color as in the photo? Thank you. Let me fix the photo. The shirt didn't fit like it was supposed to? *That's serious.* For an online business, a size large must mean the same thing every time. That's another reason I've moved to manufacturing my own apparel; I like control. Returns are tough on a small business, but we offer exchanges, because it's tougher on the woman who saved her money to shop with us, then felt let down. Exchanging showed the Chicks I cared, and because of that, they put up with more mistakes.

There were so many things that threw us off. A manufacturer missed their shipping date. I bought six—then sold eight because of software glitches. The snow. Even our best out-of-state customers forget there is one road to New Plymouth, Idaho. If it's impassable because of ice or snow, we can't ship.

Then there's the human factor. We had only been in the new store a few months before things started to slip with my shipping manager. She was arriving late. She was yelling at Morgan and Miranda (and nobody gets away with that). Things went missing. Her son was in the hospital, so I gave her a week off. Then she said she was taking the next week off for a family rafting trip. That didn't make sense. Your son is going straight from a week in the hospital to white-water rafting? I gave her the second week off, but I docked her pay.

She went ballistic. She physically attacked Justin in the shipping area. She was yelling so loudly customers in the store could hear her. She said she would take revenge on Cheekys. She said she would take revenge on my family. She said she'd help Nick make sure I never got Jack and Sterling back, because Nick was still trying to push me out of the tiny amount of time I was given. It was scary. Justin had to call the cops to remove her.

But more than that, it was sad, like heartbreaking sad. She applied for a job in the local school system, where she had worked previously, but she failed the drug test. Friends told us that, when she had relapsed eight years before, this was how she had acted. It was such a little trigger, too. She had gone to the dentist for an abscessed tooth. They gave her pain pills. Within weeks, she was out of control. And she was such a good person. I really cared for her.

But that's another thing I've learned in this business: Walking away from trouble, protecting those you are responsible for, putting them first...it's not easy, but it's necessary. Even if that means letting someone you care about go.

CHAPTER 9

THIS IS WHAT I MEAN BY HUSTLE

By 2014, Dallas was my main source of merchandise, not just Market, but Harry Hines. Unfortunately, Dallas was a three-day drive, because I still couldn't afford a plane ticket and shipping my purchases to Idaho. So I did some research and discovered a smaller market in Seattle. *That's only seven hours,* I thought. *If I start at four in the morning, I can drive there, shop for six hours, and drive back the same day. Twenty hours. It won't even require a hotel room.* The total cost was maybe a hundred dollars for gas and a sandwich. Even if I only found five good deals, the trip would pay for itself. *Let's do it!*

I took Brandie (one of my Chicks), Miranda, and Promise. This was the start of my habit of taking employees to Market with me, including the big ones in Las Vegas, Denver, and Dallas. They help with the work. They give me opinions. They find interesting buys. On the last day, we race around Market for fourteen hours, buying, packing, and loading auction items. It's the most labor we do in a single day all year.

But that's not why I take them. I could hire locals to box and pack for less. I take them so I can get to know them, as people, not just employees, and so they can learn. I don't hire someone just to squeeze labor out of them; I want them to grow. Maybe that means they learn our business and work their way up in Cheekys, or maybe that means they become confident enough to leave for a job more suited to their talents and dreams. Either way is fine with me. It's like the Cheekys Chicks. I brought you in to help me, but my goal is to help you discover who you are and what you can be.

The trip to Market doesn't work out for everyone. In early 2017, I sent a group to Vegas and came a day behind. The three-day drive is exhausting, so I bought everyone dinner and drinks when I arrived. One girl got so drunk she started making fun of another girl's weight and bra size.

The next day I sat down with her and the manager she had insulted. At the end of the meeting, I handed her a plane ticket and said, "I'm sending you home. I expect you to be gone by the time we get back. That doesn't mean I dislike you. It means I can't tolerate your behavior."

Maybe you think I should have given her another chance. I disagree. I have an "I don't care if you make mistakes, I care how you handle your mistakes" policy, both for myself and my employees. But when I see a real problem, I take care of it. I expect my girls to be kind to one another. If that's who she was, even drunk, she wasn't for Cheekys.

I had no such concerns about Brandie, Miranda, and Promise. They were good Chicks, good friends, and hard workers.

But they were local girls. All they'd ever seen was a small store in a small town. I wanted them to experience Market, so they'd understand how enormous the boutique world was. Pictures were one thing; being in the middle of 50,000 buyers swarming a million wholesale items was different. It was terrifying and exciting, in that order. Market had helped me focus on my style, pricing, and customer service, because it made me realize the competition was fierce, so I had to be my best every day. I wanted my girls to have that experience. I wanted them to see how much world there was outside Idaho and know they could still kick butt.

That didn't happen in Seattle. Or at least not how I planned. Dallas had more than 2,300 permanent vendors and ten times that many temporary booths. Seattle had, maybe, a hundred vendors at best. The crowds were so sparse, I felt like I could count each person. Worse, the prices were outrageous. These vendors and buyers, I realized, were smaller and less connected than I was. I could buy better stuff in Dallas for half the price. I drove back without buying a single item. Actually, I did buy some things...from a couple stores in town. My customers, after all, expected us to bring the Market home to them. I was getting pretty good at making a pile of very little look like a lot.

A few days later, Trisha caught me staring at the wall in the alley behind Cheekys. As usual, she was wearing a Cheekys cast-off, misprinted front and back.

"What you thinking, Jessi?" she said. She knew me so well.

"I'm thinking I can make money in Seattle."

I had gone as a buyer. What if I went back as a seller?

Between our original designs and my wholesale contacts in Dallas, I could offer better merchandise at better prices than anyone else and still make a profit.

"How much do you need?" Trisha asked.

"About five grand."

"I can do that," Trisha said. "I got a credit card." Trisha has always had unconditional trust in and love for me. She always sees me in a light I wish I could see myself in. Everyone needs and deserves a Trisha.

We left at midnight so we could arrive in the early morning and skip a night in a hotel. It was the same group—me, Brandie, Miranda, and Promise. It was seven hours of driving, plus three hours to set everything up. We had to bolt together a makeshift store with a horseshoe-shaped walkway, assemble the display shelves and tables Justin had built, and arrange and fill sixty apple crates with thousands of items—everything in the store and everything I could afford to order from Dallas.

We took a ten-minute break, or maybe five. Okay, fine, we were still putting the booth together when the doors opened at ten a.m. I had priced my merchandise at half what I would charge at retail, a fair wholesale price but twice what I'd paid in Dallas. Still, we had the best prices at the show. As the day went on, word of mouth spread, and sales increased. We had colorful winter headbands, and a group of boutique owners from Alaska bought them by the dozen. We had charm scarves dripping with big bling that, in hindsight, were hideously ugly, but I was taking orders six at a time. A man couldn't get enough of our winter boots, which looked like Uggs, Western style.

"I'll take a pair," he said. Then he sat down on our spare chair and put them on.

"They are so comfortable," he said. "I absolutely love them. I'm gonna tell everyone to go to the Cheekys booth for these amazing boots." Then he strolled off, and I could see him stopping people and pointing to his feet.

We didn't have the heart to tell him the boots were for women. We'd thought he was buying them for his wife.

Near the end of the day, I overheard a seller complaining, "This show is terrible. These people aren't even retailers. They're just the general public."

General public! What!? The traffic was so slow, the show company was letting in the folks from the dental and health insurance conventions. So I turned to Brandie, Promise, and Miranda. "Girls, we've got work to do."

That night, we raised the price of every item in our booth to just shy of retail. There were hundreds of items to sticker, so it took hours. Everyone was gone except security, who thought we were crazy. We got to the hotel after midnight, and remember, we'd left Idaho at midnight the night before. I would have bought them all a beer, but the bar was closed, and they weren't old enough to legally drink anyway. Instead we went back to our rooms—shared doubles—and straight to sleep.

The next day, our booth was packed. The booth across from us was vacant, so we expanded into it, too. Soon, the crowd was so large we blocked the aisle. It didn't matter that our prices were 25 percent higher than the day before, our sales kept climbing. And now, when licensed retailers came to the booth, I pulled them aside and said, "Everything is priced at retail, but for store owners we have a special price code in the corner of the tag. There is no minimum today, but if you decide to buy in bulk, we would be happy to make you an even better deal." Just like that, our old price became a secret sale!

We sold everything. And I mean everything. When our stock was gone, we sold our samples. We sold our signs. We sold every display shelf Justin had built. Every other wholesaler was complaining, but we identified an opportunity and left with nothing but my pink trailer (sorry, not for sale), our pricing gun, a broom, and the cash register.

I got a call two days later. It was the manager of the wholesale apparel market in Portland, Oregon. He said, "I heard what happened in Seattle. We never thought a *Western* store would do so well. Will you come to Portland?"

"I don't think so." I was tired.

"We'll give you a substantial discount."

"Hmm, okay. When's the show?"

"This weekend."

Oh, lord, I did not want to do that. But a small business can't pass up opportunities, so I went straight into another week of twenty-hour days. Instead of paying Trisha back, I rolled her loan and my profit into new merchandise. I bought everything I could get shipped from Dallas the same day. I packed it. Justin and a friend built another dozen displays and rounded up another fifty apple crates. This time, Miranda and I worked the show, and I had learned a valuable lesson in Seattle. I priced everything at full retail, with a second line code on the tags with the retailer's discount in case this show was like the last one. It was, but my margins were higher and our work days finished earlier (if you don't count the sales I was doing at night in the hotel room from my laptop). Once again, we sold everything, including Justin's new displays. Trisha got her money back with a little extra, two whole weeks before the credit card bill was due.

About a week later, I got *another* call from the coast. It was the manager of Rietdyk's Milling Company in Ridgefield, Washington. She said: "Hey, Jessi, not sure if you remember us...we were the crazy purse ladies?! I just wanted to let you know that we bought one of your displays and a screw fell out of one of the hinges. I think you might want to use a stronger hinge next time."

"I can fix that," Justin said. So he built a new display, and we shipped it to them.

Lucy Hegge, the co-owner of Rietdyk's with her husband, Don, called as soon as it arrived. "You didn't have to do that," she said. "We know things happen. We probably broke it our-selves bringing it back from the show. We just wanted to make sure you were aware of the problem in case there was a design flaw."

"Well, we needed to do it," I said. "We're not okay with sell-ing faulty merchandise. That's not what Cheekys is about."

"You know," Lucy said, "we have a retail show up here in a few weeks. Do you guys want to come? We'll buy the booth and man it, if you fill it up."

No, I did not want to come. I was exhausted. I had nothing to put

in the booth and barely enough money to try to come up with any-
thing. The last thing I wanted was to spend another weekend away
from home, away from Addy and Hunter and . . .

"Yes, thank you. We'd love to come."

It was a huge state horse expo near the ocean on the
Washington-Oregon border. There were plenty of saddles, tack,
and tools, but we were the only women's apparel and accessory
booth. And we were busy. Really busy. After a while, Don and
Lucy just sort of sat back and watched Justin and me work.

"Do you want to go to dinner?" Don asked near the end of the
show.

No, we didn't want to go to dinner, because it was probably going
to be steak or something expensive like that, and Justin and I were
dead broke. In fact, we were planning to drive home seven hours
immediately after the show so we wouldn't have to pay for a hotel.

"That would be fantastic," I said. "Thank you."

Fate intervened. Don and Lucy had a conflict, and we had
dinner at a diner with their manager, Suzie, and her husband,
Rory. Justin and I shared a plate, drank water, and prayed the
card cleared, which it did, thank goodness. I didn't want them
to know we were poor.

A few weeks later the phone rang again. It was Lucy. "I'd like
to come check out your store," she said.

Oh, no. Oh, hell no.

You have to understand, Rietdyk's was amazing. Lucy's
grandfather founded it almost a hundred years ago, and it was
on a lovely country road in a perfectly maintained stone building
alongside the Columbia River. It was primarily a farm store. It

sold feeders, animal supplies, muck boots, tools, and beautiful flower baskets. But the lighting was exceptional; the shelves colorful; the aisles immaculate. It had a mill, an actual old-fashioned hand-built grist mill that was Lucy's grandfather's original business. They ground corn and oats, mixed it with molasses from a massive vat, and sold it in the store. That's how cool Rietdyk's was. It was so beautiful, people held weddings there.

And Cheekys? I was proud of Cheekys, but it was no Rietdyk's.

So I said, "We'd love to have you, but be warned. There's no motel in New Plymouth. There is no motel in the next couple towns, either. You'll have to stay about thirty minutes away." Sadly, I was hoping it might deter them.

Lucy showed up a few weeks later with Suzie, her manager and best friend since high school. Lucy ran Rietdyk's and Suzie was her right hand, but you would never know which one was the boss. They acted equal in everything, and they clearly loved each other's company. Justin and I showed them the store and our printing "facility" (the metal storage shed). There was no air-conditioning in the shed, and it was boiling. But if Lucy and Suzie were bothered, they never showed it.

After the tour, we took them to the Double Diamond, where they serve good steaks and an excellent burger. Also, it's the only sit-down restaurant in town.

"What wines do you have?" Suzie asked the waitress.

"Red and white."

"What kind of white? Chardonnay?"

"I don't know. It comes in a white box. The other comes in a red box."

"Oh, okay. I'll have the red."

We were lucky. It was goat-roping night. Brent, the previous owner of the saloon, had built a little chute in the alley alongside the building. The goats would run through it and into a miniature roping ring in the back room, complete with a dirt floor and low railing. Sometimes the goats escaped and ran around the bar, but this is ranch country. New Plymouth may have only 1,500 people, but we know how to rodeo. One of the best bull riders in the world, Roscoe Jarboe, is from here. The patrons of the Double Diamond took their roping so seriously some brought special goat ropes. One New Year's Eve the snow was so thick the goats couldn't make it, but nobody wanted to cancel, so they roped chickens. The goats were almost always taken to the ground in a professional manner, without incident, except for a few scuffles among the spectators along the railing. Things got rowdy on goat-roping night, in the best possible way.

"Is this approved by the health commission?" Suzie said, with mock concern.

"I think we better call PETA," Lucy joked.

"Oh, just drink another box of wine," I said.

I was laughing, thinking, *Just go with it, Jessi. This is who you are.*

The next day, Lucy told us why she and Suzie had come to New Plymouth: they wanted to start a women's apparel section in Rietdyk's. They already had a name, the Barn Boutique. They were going to bust out a wall and build a barn in the store, similar to our booth. They wanted Cheekys to provide the clothing and accessories.

"Absolutely," I said, for the first time without any worries.

And that's how Rietdyk's became our first full-fledged, no-joke wholesale customer. There was a long chain of accidents that had to break our way, from the bust of the Seattle Market through goat-roping night, but I wouldn't call it luck.

I'd call it hard work, smart work, and caring about every detail—even the screws in our displays.

CHAPTER 10

ORIGINAL GANGSTERS

Finally! With Rietdyk's and half a dozen other wholesalers soon onboard, I was *finally* ready to take the big step all the little girls dream about, or at the least the little girls allowed to dream: design. We don't dream of selling dresses, right? We dream of *creating* them. It's the number one thing boutique owners ask me about and talk about among themselves: "How do I design my own stuff?"

It's the dream given to us right there in Genesis, when it says we were made in the image of the Creator. Well, if God is part of us, and He's the creator of the world, then being a creator is part of us, too.

It's also a nightmare.

Design is hard! Ideas are easy in your head, but to translate them to a shirt or a piece of jewelry? That small step feels like a mile. I went through a dozen freelancers trying to find people who could produce what I wanted. The reality with any business partner, whether designers, wholesalers, or shipping companies, is that most aren't right for you. They're either not good enough or your interests and talents don't align. To succeed, you have to find *the best fit for you.* That goes for husbands, too, which is why I'll take mine every day of the week, because Justin's semi-squishy dad bod fits perfectly with my no-nonsense mom-itude.

That's not the worst problem, though. The worst problem with design is right there in Genesis, too, when it says we are copies of our Creator. Lesser copies, but still *made in His image.* The fact is, to one degree or another, everything in this world is a copy. It's impossible to be 100 percent original. There is simply too much culture, coming at us too fast, for it not to affect every decision we make and everything we produce, even if only accidentally and subconsciously.

This leads to everyone's first complaint. Within a week of designing their first shirt, women are in the boutique chat groups: "So-and-so copied me!" This isn't a minor issue. These women are devastated. They feel their lives are ruined.

Most of the time, I look at the disputed shirt, and it's not a copy. Usually it's just a similar phrase, design, or color scheme. That's not only okay, it's inevitable. Just because you use red, white, and blue on a shirt doesn't mean no one else can. You weren't the first to put those colors together. Target did it twenty-five years ago. And Betsy Ross two hundred fifty.

Let it go. They say imitation is the sincerest form of flattery. I disagree. I say it's the sincerest form of asshattery. (Yes, that's a word.) I *hate* it. But if you start to feel like anything *similar* to your design (or recipe, or lifestyle choice) is infringing on your world, you'll drive yourself crazy.

This is not to say there aren't legitimate copying issues. There are. People will straight rip off your work, and it wasn't something I always handled well. You know when that boutique in Nampa took over my boot business? You know how I said I walked away? That wasn't the whole story, because before I walked away, I cursed that woman out. I said, "How can you sit at the dinner table with your children after what you've done? How can you be proud of yourself acting like this?" Her actions bothered me for months. They kind of still do.

Designing merchandise was much, much, much more of the same. I still see knock-offs of my first design, "Cowboys Lie." One of Cheekys' first hot designs said "Patsy Loretta Dolly" in a big, blocky font, each name on top of the other, taking up the entire front of a shirt. (If you don't know those names...I'm shaking my head, I can't even.) The design was so popular, other companies started selling shirts exactly like it. I thought, *That's a load of shit!* So I called my attorney. He told me to let it go.

"No," I said, "this is wrong. I'm going to fight it. I can't let this stand. What will this industry be if anyone can just take someone else's hard work and inspiration and..."*

"The legal action will cost about fifteen thousand dollars," he said.

Whoa, Nelly!

That stopped me. I had sold maybe three hundred shirts, huge for me back then. Each person who knocked me off probably sold fewer. Even if I won, I'd lose money. A lot of money. And by the time the case was settled, the design would be so old I wouldn't be featuring it anyway. Technically, I could own that phrase in that configuration, if I proved it was my original and it had never been used before. But the cost and time weren't close to worth it.

So I paid my first in-house designer, Donovan (you'll meet him later), to draw a guitar and added it to the shirt. People could sell their word-only shirt; they could even add their own guitar; but they could never match or copy Donovan's original drawing. I sell the best "Patsy Loretta Dolly" shirt on the market; a lot of people know it's a Cheekys design, and that has to be enough.

The fact is: If you have a good idea, you will be copied. Get used to it, ladies and gentlemen. That's the business.

Nah, that's life.

And it's not China, either. Boutique owners complain all the time: "The Chinese stole my design!"

Well, that knock-off might have been manufactured in China, but who told them to make it? Ninety-nine times out of ten (yes, I'm terrible at math) it was an American.

I've studied Chinese manufacturing, because I study everything. Always. Didn't I say that before? Rest assured, there are not a bunch of Chinese nationals in cubicles in Shanghai scouring the Internet looking for American designs. The Chinese are very interested in pleasing us. They want to manufacture things Americans love. But their model isn't to go out and find those designs themselves because, frankly, the Internet is endless, and people in China don't know what to look for.

Asking the Chinese to find the best designs for women in Idaho is like asking Cheekys to create shirts for housewives in the Zheijang province. (Yes, it's real. I found it on Google.) I mean: What do I know about them?

Chinese factories are waiting for an American—your neighbor, your friend, maybe your enemy—to hire them to manufacture a knock-off version of your successful design. They sell ten shirts, maybe a hundred, to the American who brought them the design. Then they make thousands more and sell them through the Internet and middlemen in places like the Dallas Market. Next thing you know, you show up at the Caldwell Nights Rodeo and the booth next to you is selling a crappy version of your "Rural American" baseball cap.

The question is: What are you going to do?

My first answer is: Don't be shy. I know girls who try to shield their best stuff for fear of it being knocked off. I say go the other way. Blast your best designs everywhere. Put them on a flag and march down Main Street at the head of the parade, waving it in as many faces as you can. That way, when it gets knocked off (and it will), everyone will at least know it's yours. There's a lot of money to be made that way.

The second answer was given to me, accidentally, by my mother. It was her abuse, after all, that stole my childhood. But I realized in my late twenties that my anger and fear were stealing even more. I was giving her extra years of my life, because I couldn't let go. I thought: *How much are you going to let that woman take from you, Jessi? When are you going to be the boss of your own life?*

You can't live free when you're angry. That's a hard truth. And you can't create when you're worried.

I see almost everything people copy from Cheekys. I have so many friends in the industry that very little slips past us. I get six to ten messages every day from people alerting me to design infringement. I don't get angry, but I also don't let it go. Instead, I remember the wisdom of my mentor, Chris Robin, who came into my office at the car dealership one morning and snapped, "You got to take your high heel off your employees' throats, J. D. If you give them a chance to talk, you might learn something."

So that's what I do. If someone infringes on me, I call them. I don't accuse. I ask questions, and I listen to what they have to say. Ninety percent of the time, it's a misunderstanding. They didn't know it was my design, or they didn't understand they weren't allowed to do what they did. I've made a lot of friends and received a lot of public apologies, because I handled it in a personal manner.

Here's another hard truth: If you're creating and selling a product that retails for more than fifty dollars, someone is going to knock you off and sell it cheaper. Your best option, and I'm just being practical here, is to fill the price niche below with your own cheaper version. If that doesn't fit your brand, find someone you trust to make and sell it for you, because otherwise it will be done by someone you don't know and can't control.

Cheekys isn't in that business anymore, because now we almost exclusively sell our own designs, but we used to do that a lot. Here's how two different artists approached that choice.

The first was a wonderful jewelry maker I worked with at Pink on the Dirt. She was a mom, she was a ton of fun—we hit it off. She hand-made jewelry out of her house, and I thought her sassy Western gypsy style was perfect for Cheekys. So I invited her to New Plymouth to talk about working together. Her retail was around seventy-five dollars; I thought I could mass produce and sell versions of her pieces at my target retail price of less than twenty-five dollars.

I showed her a sample I had recently received from a wholesaler trying to win my business. The piece was clearly inspired by her work, and it was being offered to me cheap. I didn't mean to threaten or scare her. I just wanted her to understand that, whether we worked together or not, people were already undercutting her market.

She was horrified. I was considering carrying the piece, but after seeing her reaction, I decided against it. I don't think she got that message, because she never returned my calls or texts.

Three years later, we got our wires crossed. She thought she was texting a different Jessi; I thought I was texting someone else with her name; and in the course of our surprisingly long confused text exchange she ended up venting: "Don't even get me started on Cheekys."

I knew it was going to hurt. There were already tears in my eyes. At one point, I considered this woman a friend. But I texted back: "Actually, this is Jessi from Cheekys. Can I ask you what I did? I honestly don't know and I want to fix this."

It took her a few hours to respond, but when she did, she *blasted* me. She said I was heartless, immoral, and cheap. She said vultures like me stole from artists who poured their heart and soul into their work. She said my shipping was bad. She said she heard terrible things about me from former employees.

Now, I've had more than forty employees through Cheekys. I'd say 90 percent of them like me, or at least we parted with a mutual understanding and respect. But several left on bad terms, like the store manager who attacked Justin. Another guy started missing shifts. Then we found him literally asleep on the job. One Sunday morning, I walked in on an employee having sex in Justin's print shop. He was having an affair, and he was using Cheekys to hide it from his live-in girlfriend. He wasn't going to tell her that, so he filed an OSHA complaint saying our unsafe work environment caused him to lose his job. Nothing came of it, but he still talks bad about me.

That's the way it is. Like with the accusations of drugs and abuse, if people want to believe the worst of me, the material is out there. Most of it's a lie, but what does that matter? This woman wanted to hate me, so she repeated those terrible rumors back to me like they weren't just true, but *the only truth* that mattered about Jessica Dawn Roberts as a businesswoman, mother, and human being.

I wasn't angry, but I was deeply hurt. I dwelled on her comments for weeks; honestly, I haven't gotten over them. But I wrote her back within half an hour (after spending the first twenty minutes crying). And I apologized. I made the first mistake in our relationship when I showed her the knock-off bracelet, and I told her that. But I also told her I never carried the bracelet. And I had never knowingly taken an artist's work, not from her or anyone else. And I was so sorry that I had hurt her.

We made up. A little. I hope she isn't angry at me anymore, and I feel better knowing what happened between us. My door is open, but from the way she left the text exchange, I doubt we'll speak again.

I still like her. I want her to succeed so much. She's a mother and a small business owner in a rural part of the world, and I want every woman like that to succeed. I know a lot of her anger was frustration that her pieces were being knocked off, and even though I'm not carrying those knock-offs (I don't think; it's impossible to research every piece), other shops are. I know she blames people like me for her struggle to reach her goals.

But the fact is, it's next to impossible to live off handmade jewelry. The process is too slow, the competition too fierce, and the profit too small. That's a side hustle, not a career. If you think you'll get rich, or even make $50,000 a year, you've set yourself up for failure, because even at a hundred dollars per piece, that would mean making and selling 500 pieces a year, and that's an unrealistic goal.

Here's a different version of that story, about a woman named Kaitlyn, whose friend gave her one of our shirts. She liked it so much, she turned our trademarked phrase into a piece of jewelry. That's not allowed. But when Kaitlyn found out she'd broken the rules, she did the right thing: She called us. So I went to her Facebook page to see who she was. That's one of the great things about Facebook; you can see me, but I can also see you.

She wasn't a large producer or even a store. She was a young mom running a small home-based business. So I called her and said, "I'm sorry, Kaitlyn, you can't use our design without approval. But I love the piece. I'd like to talk with you about mass-producing it for Cheekys."

She was skeptical. Retail is too often a bigger-fish-eats-the-little-fish business, and there are plenty of horror stories. But we talked honestly, and Kaitlyn thought, *What's the risk? It's only one design.* So we worked out a deal. I would pay her a percentage on each factory-produced version I sold, but I would also attribute the design to her and tag her in the post so the Cheekys Chicks could find her. I didn't have to do that. The design was mine. I could have just mass-produced the piece without her. But that's not Cheekys. We protect ourselves, but we're not in the business of hurting others.

The relationship worked. Kaitlyn sold her handmade original to a Cheekys Chick for about fifty dollars, and I sold close to a hundred of the factory-produced version for around fifteen dollars. Nobody got rich, but everybody came out ahead.

So I called Kaitlyn. "I like some of your other designs. Want to try it again?"

I produced three of her designs. Then five. Finally, Kaitlyn said, "Whatever you want, Jessi, I'm in." I didn't carry everything she offered—remember my first rule, only sell what you like—but for a few years Cheekys was almost always offering a couple of Kaitlyn's designs in different colors. The Chicks loved them, and since I attributed every piece to her, and I tagged her every time her jewelry was in a video or photo, they loved her, too.

I didn't make millions off this relationship. I doubt I sold a thousand of any one piece, because it's *really* hard to sell a thousand of anything (except our ridiculously popular sequin pocket scoop t-shirts). That's a fallacy in the thinking of designers. They assume a place like Cheekys "steals" their ingenious design and makes a million dollars. Sorry, girls, but there's no ingenious design worth a million dollars to a retailer like Cheekys. I'm big enough now that I might make ten or fifteen thousand off a piece, but that profit only pays my business expenses for a day. It's the *volume* of designs that makes Cheekys work. I make my numbers by working with a dozen people like Kaitlyn and, as of now, five in-house designers. They earn a good living not by hitting the jackpot, but by working hard to produce a bunch of solid designs.

Kaitlyn is out of the business now. She and her husband live in an expensive part of California, so she ultimately had to go back to work full-time. But the support of Cheekys helped keep her family afloat during a critical time in their young lives. It allowed Kaitlyn to make money during her pregnancy and spend three years at home with her infant daughter. Three years! That's a gift I'd give every woman if I could, and Kaitlyn earned it.

It hurts when people call me a vulture and accuse me of stealing their art or their market. It's frustrating when they think I'm rich, and that they'd be rich, too, if only I hadn't ruined their chance.

But then there's Kaitlyn, and the dozens of Cheekys partners like her. They don't make me rich, but they make me proud. I'd rather know I helped an amazing woman like Kaitlyn than make a million dollars any day.

But let's be honest: I'd really like to do both.

Cowgirl Justice, the company that "cattle-branded" the back of their shirts, had a top a few years back that said, "Whiskey Bent and Hell Bound." I kind of loved it. Since Cowgirl Justice only makes clothing, I asked a freelance designer to put it on a bracelet for me.

Yes, I "stole" their phrase. But Cowgirl Justice had "stolen" it from a Hank Williams Jr. song and album from 1979. If you look on the Internet, you'll find a dozen companies selling WB & HB items, from shirts to wooden signs to "Whiskey Bent and Veil Bound" tank tops designed for hard-drinking bachelorette parties in Gatlinburg, Tennessee. Miranda Lambert wore a version by a company called License to Boot.

I didn't know any of that. I just saw the Cowgirl Justice version, saw an opportunity in bracelets, and called a freelance designer. We rejected her first dozen designs, but then she came back with a beautiful script. I knew immediately that was the one, so I bought the design from her and sent it out to have ten dozen bracelets made. The decision took five minutes, tops. That's how fast it happens.

An item like that typically nets about $1,000 profit for Cheekys. If I call a staff meeting to make a decision about it, and pay five people to sit around debating it, that's a big chunk of my profit right there.

In this case, my speed burned me, because when the bracelets came in, I realized the designer hadn't created her own font, like I asked her to. Out of frustration over the rejected designs, she used the Cowgirl Justice font.

Now I had a problem. I really had stolen a competitor's design. So what should I do?

I have a saying about relationships: "Someone is going to make the first mistake." It's inevitable. If they make it, it's my duty to forgive. If I make it, it's my obligation to apologize and set it right.

Well, I'd just made the first mistake in my relationship with Cowgirl Justice, so I called them. I didn't know Kurt and Jamise Fisher, the owners. I had only admired them from afar. But I explained to Kurt who I was and what happened, and I asked what he wanted me to do. Destroy my stock? Give them the jewelry? Pay them for their design?

He laughed. "I can't believe you called to tell me that," he said. He'd been in the business a long time; he knew what I'd done was standard practice for wholesalers. But that's not Cheekys.

(continued)

He didn't want anything. They didn't do jewelry, Kurt said, so my bracelet wasn't competition. He just asked me to tag Cowgirl Justice in the posts, since by this time Cheekys was bigger than they were.

"And send me one," he said. "For my wife."

Would it have been different if I hadn't called? Probably not. They probably wouldn't have noticed my mistake. But because of my honesty, I not only had a clean conscience, I had a personal relationship with a couple I had always admired, and who turned out to be the great people I always hoped they would be.

CHAPTER 11

FIND A SUZIE

Lucy Hegge from Rietdyk's has been a mentor to me in more ways than she knows. I look up to her, because she is a funny, kind, and understanding woman. She's *Pretty*, but she knows what she wants, and she gets it, without hurting anyone's feelings. Her "Barn Boutique" is perfect for her store, because she understands what to stock and why. I value my relationship with all my wholesale customers. I give them advice whenever they ask. With good customers like Lucy, it's a two-way street, because I learn from them, too.

She has a great marriage. She and Don are still laughing and enjoying each other's company after forty years of living and working together. They throw an incredible Halloween party in Portland in an old restored barn, and one year Justin and I were lucky enough to attend. Not only that, Lucy and Don let us stay on their boat. Okay, it's not a boat, it's a freaking yacht, although they'd never call it that. They are extremely humble. Well, Lucy is, anyway.

When Justin asked how they afforded the boat, Don said, "We traded up."

They started with a little ski boat twenty-five years ago, and they kept making deals until they ended up with one of the biggest boats on the Columbia River. Guess who has a $1,400 fishing skiff on a trailer in the backyard right now? We haven't traded up. We haven't even put it in the water in more than a year because we're so busy. But Justin continues to dream. He sold his mini-tractor and camper to help Cheekys, but nobody is touching his starter yacht!

The best piece of advice Lucy ever gave me, though, was, "Find yourself a Suzie."

Find someone you trust to be your right hand. Someone you love being around, who makes you happy you're alive and confident in your decisions. (That's where husbands fail; they tend to question, not reassure.) Someone you'd feel comfortable running the business in your absence, however long that might be.

I gave you the same advice in chapter 1. You probably didn't take it seriously, because you know what? I didn't take it seriously when Lucy gave it to me. I mean, who wouldn't want a Suzie? Suzie was great. But was she necessary?

Then I had an accident.

When I was four, I was playing in the collapsed storefront next to the strip club while W worked on some old trashed trailer he'd picked up for nothing. He had a big sheet of wood with a knothole in it, and he called me over.

"I need help," he said. "Look through that knothole for me."

I pressed my eye right up to the hole…and he shoved the end of a coat hanger into it. It hurt so bad. I was on the ground thrashing and crying. W was laughing. He thought that was hilarious, stabbing a kid in the eye. Mom came out, and they started arguing. They never took me to the doctor, so I lost the peripheral vision in my left eye.

That's why I didn't see the toolbox sitting outside Justin's backyard workshop. I had been running the auction site, came out for a break, tripped over the toolbox, and took a header straight into the concrete.

I blacked out, and when I woke up I had a broken nose and a headache so bad I couldn't open my eyes. When I finally managed to open them, in the hospital, everything was fuzzy. I saw multiple versions of everything: five Addys, four Hunters, two dozen Justins. It wasn't my eyes, the doctors told me; I had a brain hemorrhage made worse by the damage from numerous undiagnosed concussions I must have suffered as a kid.

"Bring me my computer," I told Justin when we got home.

"Jessi, that's not a good idea."

"I have to, Justin," I said. "I have to answer Facebook posts. I have to ship."

I tried looking at my phone, but the light from the screen was a knife in my brain. "One day off," I said.

The next morning, a massive purple bruise covered the entire left side of my face. My forehead and cheek were so swollen I didn't look like myself. Here's the picture, because it's worth a thousand words:

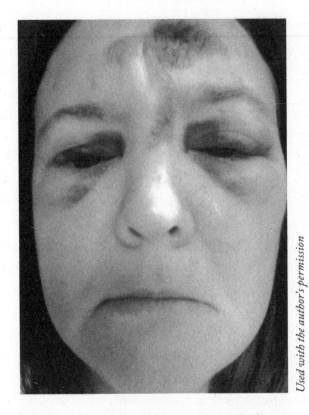

Used with the author's permission

I tried to work anyway, but it was torture to look at a screen.

"You have to rest, Jessi," Justin said.

But who is going to run Cheekys?

My girls could handle the store, but what about my 10,000 Facebook followers? This was a few months after signing Riet-dyk's. I had maybe twenty solid wholesale customers. It was a potentially lucrative business. It was the future of Cheekys. But what if no one was there to service them? There were plenty of other designers and boutiques. What if all my contacts left before I could get that business off the ground?

The best way I can describe Cheekys is like a stagecoach. Justin's the driver; I'm the horse. I'm gonna run 'til I drop; that's who I am. It's Justin's job to rein me in when my ambition gets ahead of reality. He's great at that. He's great at building stuff. He's pretty great at printing shirts, too. But he can't pull this business, because he can't manage store relationships and run an active Facebook page about women's jewelry and apparel.

"Don't worry," Justin said. "Trisha's taking care of things."

Trisha. My best friend. My Suzie. The day I hit my head, she came to my house. That night, she took over the Cheekys Facebook page without being asked. She kept things on schedule with my wholesale customers. She drove from Oregon to New Plymouth every day to make sure Morgan, Miranda, and my newest employee, Dana, were keeping the store tip-top. She ran things her way, because Trisha always did things her way. She didn't hang with the staff; she didn't chat and emoji with the Chicks; she wasn't accommodating like me. Some customers didn't like that, but Trisha didn't care. When they complained, she said, "I don't work for Jessi. I'm a partner in this business, so what I say goes."

I was out for six weeks. Perhaps that seems...nice? After all, fighting the custody battle, founding the Cheekys Chicks, closing the Nampa store, relocating the original store, and pouring all my time and money into creating and manufacturing my own designs weren't short-term events that happened one after the other. They overlapped, bleeding from one to the other and back again. For years, I had been working nonstop, even as I was crying myself to sleep every night over Jack and Sterling. Surely I deserved a rest, right?

This was no rest. I lay awake in a dark room, trying to keep my head from splitting open. My poor children had to tiptoe around the house, because noise set off a migraine. Even four weeks after the accident, I couldn't type. The letters came out jumbled. The doctors said the fall had unhooked my brain from my motor functions. Recovery took time.

I hated it. My family has a bad history with addiction. Granny Dee was an alcoholic. Mom's life fell apart over inhalants and champagne, and if you think that doesn't sound *that* bad, think again. I inherited Daddy Joe's weakness: I was addicted to work. That's not healthy, but unlike alcohol or drugs, at least you come out with something worth having in the end.

It means, however, that I drove myself crazy thinking about work, and I drove Justin crazy, too. If I couldn't work, and I couldn't type, and I couldn't look at a screen, at least let me talk, Justin!

He said, "Jessi, relax. Drink this Clamato juice. Let me take care of you for once."

And I did, finally. I relaxed, focused on myself and, thanks to Trisha, Cheekys carried on fine. There were a few twisted hairs, but I doubt even the most enthusiastic Chicks remember my 2014 "vacation" now. Only a few people know I was injured. Today, I would post the gruesome pics. I would get so much love back from the Chicks, and we'd have a great laugh. But back then, I was anxious. I didn't have confidence in myself. I thought customers would leave me if they found out I was weak. The photo included here is the first time I have shown pictures of that incident to anyone.

Not long after I returned to work, Trisha moved away. She and her husband bought a two-room hut on a mountain in Hawaii and retired for good. (I've never visited her, but one of these days.) She still runs Cheekys Auctions, and I still only pay her $1,200 a month. She cashed out most of her ownership in Cheekys for almost no profit, at her insistence. But even if it was a heap of cash, how could it be enough, after all she's done for me?

Trisha helped me recover from a serious car accident. She helped me raise Hunter. She helped me through my pregnancy when I was alone. Whenever I doubted myself, she said, "Do what you think is right, Jessi. You're smart. You know what you're doing." She was my Suzie. She saved Cheekys when I was hurt, and there was no one else to step in and keep the company going.

So thanks. Trisha, my bestie-for-life. I have a misprinted shirt with the cover of this book on it, waiting for you.

CHAPTER 12

SURVIVING THE BULL SHIRT

I was at the Las Vegas Market in the spring of 2014, buying and packing my pennies-on-the-dollar items on the last day of the show, when a man asked what I was doing.

"That's smart," he said, when I explained my auction business.

He asked about my background. I told him I owned a Western-focused apparel company named Cheekys. He told me he was a wholesaler and manufacturer. He designed some Western items. Would I give him my opinion?

I never pass up an opportunity to learn, so I went. He had a huge permanent booth, one of the largest at the Vegas Market. But I would never buy his stuff, and I told him that.

"Why?"

"Well, that horse only has three legs," I said, pointing to a faux leather purse. "That horse doesn't have a mane. That one looks like a giraffe."

On one piece, there was a cartoon drawing. Above it, one

word: "Horse." Like somebody wouldn't know! I mean, the art was terrible, but still.

And then there were the mistakes. "Hell on Heecs," a bracelet said, instead of "Hell on Heels." Another said: "chicken laddy."

Honestly, it wasn't a surprise. A lot of wholesalers were trying to crack the Western market, but their quality was spotty and their designs were *awful*. They were farming out the work to cut-rate overseas designers, and those poor people couldn't even get the mountains right, because they'd never seen the Rockies. They messed up cactuses. "Indian prints" looked like they were from Mumbai, not the Navajo. And the animals! Bulls with udders. Horses with no ears. Animals I couldn't identify, but... sheep? Or goats. Or elephants.

That was one of the first design rules I laid down with Cheekys: All our animals will be anatomically correct. We don't make cartoon animals. We don't confuse males and females. A horse isn't a "horse"; we know the breed. I have a chicken *mansion* in my backyard, for God's sake. My family has raised pigs, goats, and cows, both heifers and bulls. I know the difference between a Plymouth Rock and a Rhode Island Red, and so do my customers.

"Being Western and rural is a lifestyle," I said. "We care about this stuff. It's in our blood. Sorry, but that's never gonna sell. We can spot a fake a mile away."

He nodded, like he was seeing his errors—three-legged horse, y'all!—for the first time. A few weeks later, he called me. "Let's talk," he said.

He flew Justin and me to Arizona. He put us up in his multi-million-dollar mansion. He owned two factories in Asia, he explained, and had thousands of retail clients across the United States. He could manufacture, and he could sell. But he needed better products for the Western market, and he wanted us to design them.

He offered us $8,000 a month, for six months, and a percentage of sales. He would own the designs but allow us to sell versions under the Cheekys label. And he would give Cheekys a booth at the Denver Market to raise our national profile.

It was my dream come true. I needed more wholesale customers. I needed more manufacturing contacts. I needed more money, period, because we had to pay for items up front and Cheekys kept getting turned down for a line of credit from a bank. Some items, even when I believed in them, I simply couldn't afford to produce.

Q was offering a solution to all these problems. He could streamline my ordering process, standardize my manufacturing, pay my up-front expenses, and open my products to a giant new market. In short, he could make Cheekys a big-deal brand.

And $8,000 a month? With that kind of money, my family would be financially secure, and I would have enough to fight for custody of Jack and Sterling. With my percentage, if the designs hit, I might make millions. I told you not to dream of millions, right? Well, it's hard to resist. I was dreaming of millions!

So we shook hands on a deal. The contract would take time, but I didn't want to wait. Q was offering the chance of a lifetime—a chance I'd earned, but still, I was appreciative. I put the New Plymouth store into Morgan, Miranda, and Justin's hands and devoted myself to design.

The first thing I did was offer Donovan half of Q's monthly payments to work for Cheekys full time. Donovan was Justin's designer, film output service, screen-maker, and ink supplier in Portland. He had visited us in New Plymouth, and Justin had visited him several times in Portland, including for a weeklong class that finally got him cranking out shirts at a decent pace. That and a used six-over-six press Justin found for a good price. The man does love his machines.

Donovan was also my best freelance designer. So I told him, "I'm not looking for precious. I don't want you getting possessive. We're going to work together, and we're going to work fast. We're going to knock out three or four designs a day." That's my style. Get it done. Get it right. Get it sold. What are you waiting for?

Donovan accepted my offer and moved to New Plymouth.

Actually, he moved into my house. Justin had finally finished the living room, after a year of plastic sheeting and bare studs, although the kitchen cabinets are even now only about 90 percent. He built three bedrooms for the boys in the basement, and since Jack and Sterling rarely used theirs, Donovan stayed in one while he looked for a place to rent.

Justin had also enclosed the wraparound porch, so that's where Donovan and I worked. It was crowded, since I had already outgrown my shipping area in New Plymouth and was storing hundreds of auction items out there, but I've always felt more comfortable in the center of the storm. That's a personal thing. I wouldn't advocate messiness. But for me, it was comfortable to get up in the morning, get my coffee, and get to work in the middle of my random stacks of merchandise.

I don't want you to think that because we worked fast, we worked sloppy. We did the same amount of design work on each piece as everyone else, we just cut out all the sitting around. I threw out an idea; Donovan created a basic design. Then we started experimenting. What if we changed that color? What if we added stars? What if we threw the word "darlin'" into the mix? (I like the word "darlin'.") What if, what it, what if…

Donovan was a new experience for me. After all, he was from *Portland*. He wore skintight jeans, garage printed punk tees, with full sleeve tattoos and half a pompadour like a 1950s greaser. When we went into Garbonzo's pizza, three doors down and the only restaurant in New Plymouth besides the Double Diamond and the burger joint, everyone assumed he was gay.

"He's just metro." I laughed. "Lots of straight guys get manicures."

I guess.

Donovan had a cooler-than-you vibe, Portland style. I realize now that's mostly insecurity, because the flip side of "cool" is a constant worry the work is not cutting edge, someone is better, and you are *falling behind*. But his restlessness and anxiety didn't bother me. I'm an anxious person, too. I mean, any second my customers might decide Cheekys wasn't cool, right? There are a million prettier girls they could buy from, right? That shared insecurity drove us to be better. Donovan was the first person I worked with who matched my energy. We stayed up until midnight many, many nights, knocking out designs.

We worked all through the spring and early summer. That's the nicest time of year in Idaho. The late summer is dry and hot, and the frequent brush fires can blot out the view of the mountains for weeks. I've had mornings where the smoke from fires fifty miles away was so thick I couldn't drive the two miles to New Plymouth. The cold comes early, even if the snow usually holds off until Thanksgiving. Spring is when we take the family out for camping trips, when we drive northeast to Lost Lake, or past Lost Lake into the Sawtooth Range, or northwest to Hell's Canyon. That's when the elk come out of the mountains to forage and the steelhead travel so far up the Snake River the fishermen line the banks from the Oregon border past the Payette County line.

I missed spring that year. I was too busy working. Donovan and I were delivering designs to Q every day, and he loved them. *Yes*, he said. *Yes, yes. This is it. This is exactly what I want.* We designed everything he asked for: shirts, jeans, dresses, belts, jewelry, headbands, handbags, wallets, boots, flip-flops, hats, tin signs, logos, catalogues, and displays. You name it, we made. We probably designed 350 decorative wall crosses alone.

Nothing was getting produced, but Q had reasons. There was a backup at the factory. He was waiting for more orders. The demand was greater than expected. He wanted to make 100,000 of each piece, that's how popular they were, but working with that kind of volume took time.

I was still running Cheekys. I was engaging customers and responding on Facebook and ordering my shirts and accessories a dozen at a time. One day, I called my contact at a belt factory in China. I had met him through the son of the older Asian woman on Harry Hines, so we'd known each other a long time.

"How did your customers like those new belts?" he asked.

"What belts?"

"The two-thousand-piece order we just made."

We both realized there was something wrong at the same moment. I hadn't placed any orders, and certainly not for two thousand pieces. So he described the belts. He assumed they were my designs, since they were my style. Oh, and they were stamped with my brand.

Well, they were my designs, of course. The ones I made for Q.

But he never told me about an order for belts. Had Q forgotten to pass on the info, or was this the way it worked? And why was he working through an independent factory? Didn't Q own his manufacturing plants?

We went to the Denver Market, to the booth Q gave Cheekys as part of the deal. The space was large, but off in a corner, and when I mentioned Q, I got dirty looks. He wasn't welcome in Denver, I was told. His company was banned from the show. He had thrown us into a space he had paid for in advance but couldn't use.

Suck it up, Jessi, I thought. *Be Pretty. This will all work out.*

Then the buyers for Rod's Western Wear came breezing through. Between its popular catalogue and 20,000-square-foot store in Columbus, Ohio, Rod's is one of the largest Western retailers in the country. Their buyers swept into our space like royalty, four young women following an older woman who was clearly the queen, and started pointing at our merchandise.

"We bought that. We bought that. I recognize that."

"Someone tried to sell it to us three months ago," one of the young followers replied. "The quality was poor."

"We bought that. We passed on that."

"Those are so old," a young woman scoffed.

"We brought in that whole line of belts last summer."

They weren't talking to me. They were talking to each other. But my heart sank. They had seen my designs; they had even bought my belts. They were on their website right then, and I know that, because I checked. That's when I knew Cheekys was being robbed.

I had been victimized before. W, my "stepfather," was a violent, dangerous man. He beat me with whatever was at hand: a piece of flooring, a straightened coat hanger, a metal bar, his fists, and that's just the things I remember. He raped my mother repeatedly, mostly to keep her in line. He raped other women, too, but mainly mom, because she was his girl. Sometimes, he made me watch. He had no shame. None. The more I saw, he figured, the more I'd fear him, and to W fear was good.

When I was nine, he told me to get in his car. He had a long, low-riding Cadillac with curb feelers, a car so stereotypically pimp it feels like a joke, and he drove slow, like a shark. I knew he was looking for something, but I didn't know what. Turns out, he was hunting for a man. I can't remember the details. Did the man run when he saw the car? Did W chase him?

All I remember is a man on his knees. W was standing over him. He turned to me and said, "This is why you pay your debts." Then he shot the man in the face.

W didn't say he would kill me if I told anyone about the murder. He didn't have to. W always said he was going to kill me eventually, sometimes angrily and sometimes with a laugh, and I believed him. He broke my bones. He tried to drown me, the only time I was ever taken to the hospital. He liked to hold me and beat me with a cane until I was bruised to the bone. Then he would release me, and I would collapse. I still have scars on my knees and hands from the broken glass.

He owned abandoned houses. They had no plumbing or electricity, but he'd installed window bars and door locks that only opened from the outside. His favorite punishment was to strip me naked and lock me in one of those houses with nothing but a bag of oranges and an empty bucket for a bathroom. Usually, he left me three days. Sometimes more. There was nothing in those houses but mildew and spiders. I sat on the bucket all night, listening to the rats and praying for morning, because then mom might rescue me. But mom never came.

Even as a little girl, I understood that I was going to die in one of those houses, and nobody would miss me, and my body would never be found. But W would to have to kill me, I told myself, because I would never give up.

I've never told Justin any of this, or my children. I told my first husband, Ben, a little, but he didn't understand until we went to my mother's house. This was years later, and she was living with a different man. Mom pulled out a scrapbook with pictures of me from about age two to eight. She was trying so hard. *Look, wasn't Jessi cute? Look, we took pictures. We were a normal family.*

"Oh, my God. Jessi," Ben said, when we were out in the driveway. "I am so sorry. I didn't know. You told me, but I didn't know."

I knew what he meant, because I'd seen it, too. It wasn't just that I was so often naked in those photos, which stopped me cold. It was that in every photo, even when I was two or three years old, I was terrified.

None of that helped me as an adult. It didn't make me tough. It didn't make me empathetic. Nothing good comes from abuse. Nothing. It is only evil. But if you insist I learned from those experiences, that my childhood must have contributed to my success in some way, then it was this: I was raised by con artists, grifters, criminals, and thieves. I grew up around men and women who didn't think twice about hurting other human beings, even children, so I can spot those kinds of people, no matter where they are or how they present themselves. Many people you meet in business are frauds. Some are criminals and grifters. Others are good people worth everything you put into them and more. I prided myself on knowing the difference.

But somehow, Q slipped through my defenses. He conned me for months. And when I finally caught on, like a true bastard, he tried to destroy me.

Q had given us a credit card. He told us to charge half of our $8,000 monthly retainer on it every two weeks, and to put other expenses related to our partnership on the card. Now he claimed to the card company that none of those charges were authorized, and that he had never agreed to pay us anything. We didn't have a contract. He promised one, but it never came through. He wasn't just stealing our designs. He had been planning to defraud us all along.

His first claim against us was for $48,000—all six months of payments. Cheekys had been doing well. We had almost that much money saved. But the credit card company froze our assets until they could investigate the complaints. Suddenly, I didn't have a penny. I was back to living hand-to-mouth, missing more meals than I ate so Hunter and Addy (and Jack and Sterling, on the rare occasions they were with us) never went hungry. It was devastating. I thought I was breaking through; instead, I was more broke than ever. And it wasn't just the $48,000. There were financial penalties if they ruled we had committed fraud. There was the possibility of jail time.

Oh, no, I thought, *I've destroyed Cheekys and ruined my family.*

Justin wrapped me in his arms. "We're going to beat this, Jessi," he said. "We're going to win, because we've done nothing wrong."

Q thought he was conning bumpkins, but he messed with the wrong country folks. Justin is careful about paperwork. Yes, when Cheekys started, I kept my sales records in a spiral notebook, but from day one, I wrote down every transaction. Justin checked our books every week to make sure every penny was accounted for. I tracked and recorded every order, even the ones that ultimately didn't pan out. Taxes. Payroll. Accounting. Cash flow. Keeping your book watertight isn't a luxury; it's a necessity.

So we were ready. We had sent messages to Q confirming

every partnership detail. That's called a paper trail. Justin sat down with the credit card auditor (metaphorically, since they worked by phone and email) and proved we had an agreement with Q to pay us $4,000 every two weeks, even if we didn't have a signed contract.

So Q went after the expenses. We had asked for and received Q's written authorization for every charge.

On our initial trip to his mansion, Q had hired Justin to rebuild a barn. Justin took Hunter with him for the summer, and along with Ben, they spent two months working under Q's direction. Q made a claim against the work. He said Justin was negligent because he hadn't pulled permits. He was right; Justin hadn't pulled permits. The job site was shut down. But that was Q's decision. He had claimed permits weren't necessary. Justin disagreed, so he refused to start working until Q signed a paper releasing him from liability. We won that dispute, too.

Eventually, Q stopped making claims. He realized he couldn't beat us, so he took his "loss" and moved on. It took almost four long months of Justin working on the problem every day, though, to clear our names and unfreeze our assets. He was so stressed he could barely keep down his red beer. And then, suddenly, Cheekys was free.

I learned many lessons from my misadventure with Q, none more important than the obvious: There is no shortcut. If something sounds like your dream come true, that's probably because someone is using your dreams against you. The wholesalers—the "Big Guys"—aren't our friends or partners. They don't care about little sellers like us. They're perfectly happy to put us out of business, if that's in their best interest. And to many, that's *always* in their best interest.

In fact, wholesalers are moving right now toward eliminating small retailers. Why? Because we aren't needed anymore. Wholesalers used stores like Cheekys as distribution points. It was the only way to reach customers in places like the Payette Valley. But now sales are migrating to the Internet, so there's less need for the middlewoman. Massive wholesalers are just as capable of reaching customers on the Internet as Cheekys, Mixed Mercantile, Filly Flair, and the rest of us. After all, anyone can post product on Amazon, and the profit margin is much higher going direct to consumer. The wholesalers are rushing into that market, undercutting independent retailers. As soon as they figure out how to effectively copy our Facebook pages and websites, they'll stop selling to us altogether.

That's why, after Q, I cut loose from wholesalers. He didn't mean to, but Q had taught me everything I needed to know to run a wholesale business myself. I had always been able to design the merchandise. I could reach customers. But I couldn't manufacture. That's the piece I was missing. When Q told me he owned factories, I believed him, because every wholesaler says they own factories.

They don't. That's a lie. Wholesalers have *contacts* at factories. Well, Cheekys can do that, too. The fact is, in the same way the big wholesalers don't need us, we don't need them. We're both middlemen. What's actually happening is this: Wholesalers and retailers are losing the distinction between them. The future is businesses that can do both: make their own products *and* reach consumers. It takes a large following and an even bigger hustle—otherwise you're just cheap selling—but ever since my relationship with Q fell apart in early 2015, that's what Cheekys has been doing.

I still see some of the products I designed for Q for sale in places like Hobby Lobby and Tractor Supply. There are gas stations in the Dallas–Fort Worth area that still sell decorative crosses Donovan and I designed. They are the worst quality, chintziest plastic-and-rhinestone crap, and the price is usually a couple bucks.

I guess Q is making money on it, but I don't care. I'm done with that chapter of my life. The future isn't behind me; it's ahead. Besides, I'd be embarrassed to have something that poorly made associated with Cheekys. Q did me a favor, in a way, when he sold me out.

What was I thinking, I wonder now, when I gave a man I barely knew that much control? I should have seen that mistake from the start, because the most important thing is still the most fundamental thing: Run your business your way.

Ask yourself: What is important to me?

Was my goal to make Cheekys a national brand? No. I would love that, obviously. But my goal was for Cheekys to support my family and employees. It was to produce quality products for rural women and sell them at a fair price. I wanted Cheekys to stand for what is good about country life: honesty, hard work, and taking care of the people you love. I wanted it to inspire, encourage, and empower small-town girls around the world. If I sold out that vision to become a bigger brand, then what did I have?

Nothing.

Nothing important, anyway. That realization might have been worth almost losing everything. (Okay, it wasn't, but it lessens the sting.)

That's not the end of this story, though. Shortly after Q broke our arrangement by accusing Cheekys of fraud, I saw a necklace that said, "That's bullshit, darling." Maybe I was in the mood. Maybe it captured what I was thinking at that moment. I loved it.

The saying felt a little aggressive, though, like pointing a finger. I don't like pointing fingers. So I started brainstorming. Could we make it more Cheekys? Could I find a phrase that was ornery and strong, without being confrontational? Eventually, I hit on "Don't bullshit me, darlin'." It felt like attitude with a smile.

I said, "Donovan, we have a drawing of a bull somewhere, don't we?"

I gave him the phrase and the font I wanted. He came back in fifteen minutes. Honestly, that's all it took to create a design with DBSMD, in a handwritten script, on the side of a very realistic black-and-white bull.

Donovan said, "I just wanna make a few changes. Maybe try a different font."

"Nope," I said, "it's perfect. Let's post it and see what happens."

I had just signed up for a service called Fashion Go, a website where designers and small wholesalers can post their merchandise for a hefty fee. "Bullshit" was one of the first items I ever posted there.

Almost immediately, it was: I want three. I want ten. I want twenty.

Since Fashion Go was a closed portal for retailers, I had to post "Bullshit" on the Cheekys Facebook page to reach the Chicks. That's when I got nervous. Cheekys had attitude, but we didn't curse (in public). What would my customers think? Would they be offended? Many of my girls are Christian. Would it cost me those loyal followers? Was this the right time to take a chance like that?

I went with my gut. I loved the design, so I figured the Chicks would, too. I never anticipated how much. That's one thing you learn real fast in retail: Keep expectations low. Otherwise, you're an emotional wreck. So I was surprised when, within minutes of posting, we started getting messages: *I love this. My favorite Cheekys item ever. Right on, Jessi. This made me smile, LOL.*

What really made me smile weren't the social media notifications, though, but the payment notifications. People were buying, and buying fast.

Between Fashion Go and the Chicks, we had more than a hundred responses the first day. We sold $17,000 worth of "Bullshit" in the first week. Today, the design is one of our all-time best-sellers. We've sold more than 25,000 hoodies at $44 apiece, making "Bullshit" a million-dollar item. The 10,000 we sold that first Christmas season was enough to replenish the company bank account and launch us into our next phase, even after Q almost wiped us out.

I guess some might call it karma. We stuck to our guns; we were honest in the face of dishonesty; and we were rewarded.

Sorry, but the world doesn't work like that. It doesn't give, just because someone took. The truth is we had been cranking out great designs for a year, and the law of averages meant one would eventually break through. The fact that our biggest success happened at our darkest moment was more luck than anything else. But you make your own luck in this life, don't you, darlin'?

I've been saying *Be Pretty* a lot, and I don't want you to misunderstand that. *Be Pretty* doesn't mean *be a pushover*. There's a difference between never letting them get to you and letting them push you around. This is business. *This is life.* You gotta be a Boss Molly every now and then, or somebody's gonna eat you up.

What's a Boss Molly? Well, a molly is a female mule. The boss molly is the smartest, most stubborn mule in the herd—and yes, it's always a female. Nobody messes with a boss molly. Justin's cousin is the coolest woman on earth. She's a strong, generous, opinionated, world-class muleskinner... and no, that is not someone who takes the hides off mules. A muleskinner races mule teams. It's a fast, dangerous sport, and it takes a firm hand, because mules aren't like horses: They *hate* following your lead. Justin's cousin is smarter and more stubborn than the mollies, though. They call her the "mule whisperer" around here, because she tamed the notorious Moscow clone, the orneriest mule in Idaho. And

(continued)

yes, her name is Molly. That's what happens when your father is a four-time national champion muleskinner, too.

So what does being a Boss Molly look like IRL?

Well, I was coming out of the Caldwell Nights Rodeo last year, and a woman in front of me was so drunk she was weaving. Her husband stopped at the Cheekys booth and asked if she wanted something, probably to distract her from falling down, and she slurred, "I don't want any of that tacky shit. That shit is all shit."

Which is fine, whatever, until the woman in the booth next to us started clapping.

I turned on her and said, "What are you clapping for? Do you think that's funny? This is my business. This is how I feed my children. Just like that's your business, and that's the way you feed your children. I'm not going to clap if a drunk insults you."

She cocked her hip and said, "Well, I'm from Texas and..."

"Great. I'm from Texas, too. Where you from?"

That stopped her. She said, "Um, actually, I'm from Oregon, but..."

"Well, I don't know how you do it in Oregon, but we're all women, and most of us are mothers, and we support each other over here. If you're not interested in that, then I suggest you don't come back."

It took a minute, but she apologized. The two of us were right as rain. But Morgan, who was running the Cheekys booth that night, wasn't happy. She considers herself an expert on Cheekys, since she was my first hire, so she pulled me aside and told me that's not what Cheekys was about, and that's not how Cheekys Chicks behave.

I thought, *Excuse me, Morgan, but Cheekys is my company. I determine what Cheekys stands for.* And part of being a Cheekys Chick is standing up for yourself and others. I wasn't attacking that woman. I wasn't insulting her merchandise. I wasn't trying to hurt her or her business. That would have been wrong. But she crossed the line, so I called call her out and explained, in no uncertain terms, that her condescending attacks on other women weren't appreciated by me, or by anyone else, for that matter.

That's Boss Molly.

And you know what? That's *Being Pretty*, too.

CHAPTER 13

PICKING PARTNERS

Donovan (and his two cats) finally moved out of my house in the fall, shortly after the mess with Q was resolved. A few weeks later, my father and his wife moved in. Pops had been diagnosed with prostate cancer, motivating him to finally travel north of Amarillo and visit us in Idaho for the summer month when Jack and Sterling were with us. There isn't much in life better than camp chairs, red beer, and playing with the kids in our three-acre backyard. I think Pops saw all this life going on, and his grandkids growing up, and realized he was missing out.

It would be impossible to exaggerate how much I love this man. It wasn't his fault our life together didn't work out when I was a teenager; it was mine. But Pops loved me through everything, and I know it broke his heart to put me in the state home. After I came back to Texas with Hunter at twenty-two, he was my rock. Pops, Daddy Joe, and the whole Brooks family took me in. They protected me. They were the first people to love me for who I was. I'd fight wild dogs for every one of them, and I know they'd do the same for me.

So I worked hard to convince Pops to move to Idaho, where he could be a real part of my family, and we could take care of him through his illness. The plan was for him to work a few hours a week in the print shop with Justin, but by the time he and his wife, Jenna, arrived in early November, we had a thousand orders for "Bullshit" from retailers setting up booths at the NFR (that's the National Finals Rodeo, of course). Justin and Pops ended up working sixty hours a week for the rest of the year, and Pop swears to this day (with a smile) that he would have gone straight home as soon as the first snow fell if Justin hadn't been knocking on his door to give him a ride to work every morning.

I was glad to have the extra hands, because Cheekys was ready to expand. A lot of boutique owners want to become wholesalers. They've produced a popular shirt, or their store is profitable, or they have 100,000 Facebook followers, so they want to create, manufacture, and wholesale a line of clothing. I applaud the thought. Manufacturing and design are the future for small retailers. But my first question is always, "What's the last thing you read?"

By that I mean: Have you studied this area of the business? What do you know? If you haven't put in a hundred hours of practice and study, you aren't ready for full-scale production. That's true for any large investment, monetary, emotional, or otherwise.

My second question: "What are you prepared to lose?"

When you design and manufacture an item, you have to be prepared to lose every penny, because it's a real possibility. The manufacturer may not deliver; the final product may be wrong or, worse, ugly; it might arrive so late you miss your ship date and orders are canceled; or maybe it simply doesn't sell.

You should ask yourself that question about every big decision: "Am I prepared to lose everything I put into this? Is it worth the risk? Can I continue to live the life I want if it fails?"

Justin and I made that mistake with his industrial coating business. We spent more than we could afford to lose, and it almost cost us everything. That doesn't mean don't spend. It certainly doesn't mean don't risk. Life is risk. But ask yourself before every big decision: Is this the specific risk I want to take? Is this the right time? How far am I willing to go?

Cheekys had a strong customer base. We had a printing facility and people who knew how to run it. We had design expertise: not just Donovan, but me. I had spent three years and about 4,000 hours learning, through trial and error, what my customers wanted. I had designed every element of that "Bullshit" hoodie. And thanks to that hoodie—and the credit card company unfreezing our assets, and Justin and me paying ourselves only $2,000 a month—we had the money. Almost $100,000, the minimum to take a crack at manufacturing and wholesaling a product line. We were ready.

The biggest challenge was scaling up to factory manufacturing. Before Q, I had spent a year developing manufacturing contacts. I'm not going to tell you the specific resources I used. Sorry, my contacts are too valuable to my business. But I can tell you this: I started with the approach I used for all business arrangements. I asked questions of everyone I met. (Yes, I'm that person who always asks the waitress her favorite menu item. And I ask her follow-up questions, too. I've been a waitress. They know their business.)

If I got a good tip, for instance, from a friend at Market or another boutique owner, I researched the company on the Internet. I made calls to China and India and Vietnam, despite the language barrier and the time zone difference. Many small business owners don't like to do that. They don't want to hustle and research to find the best contacts when there's always an easier option to fill their order. Well, suck it up, buttercup, it's required. If you're not up to the time and effort of making personal connections at factories halfway around the world, don't manufacture.

If I liked a manufacturer, I placed a *minimum* order, meaning the lowest number they would run. This might be a hundred pieces for apparel, or a dozen for jewelry. If the minimum was more than I could afford, I moved on. Factories with large minimums weren't interested in smaller producers like me, so why bother?

I used my first order as a test. How responsive was the company to my needs? Did they send samples? *All good manufacturers send samples.* Was it a pain in the butt to get samples? How was the quality? If I wanted a change, how quickly and happily did they make it? Did they ever pressure me or make me feel like I was asking too much? Finally, did the order arrive on time, at the right price, in the way I intended?

When you hit the right manufacturer, you know it, just like when you find the right man. It's not even a question in your mind. After dozens of underwhelming dates, this is the special someone. Looks good. Comes through. Puts you first. Makes you feel warm and tingly inside. That's a valuable contact. Keep her close.

Q had tried to separate me from my manufacturing contacts. I can see why now, since my belt guy in China accidentally tipped me off to his scheme. But he also knew that without manufacturing, I was dependent on him.

So I went back to my old contacts. Some were easy to find. The belt guy, for instance, contacted me. He had been fired over the misunderstanding, so he was opening his own small shop, just him and his uncle. He wanted a chance to win my business. This was a loyal man who always worked hard for me. He lost his job because of me. (Well, because of Q.) So I gave him a small order. He came through, so I sent him another. He's my belt guy today.

My belt business is small. My apparel business, both finished items and blank shirts to print on, is (along with jewelry) the heart of my brand. Before Q, I worked with apparel factories all over the world, including here in America, but never felt comfortable with any of them. So when I started my own product line, I spent months looking for the right match. Nothing worked. Nobody met my quality, my price, and my level of service.

Then I stumbled onto Grace. I feel okay giving you her name, because half the women you work with in Asia are named Grace.

It's not their real name, obviously, just the one they use for doing business with English speakers. It's what they want to be for us, a grace in our lives.

I had worked with Grace on an order for hoodies before I met Q. She sent a sample, and I hated it, I don't even remember why, so I never placed the order. All I can say is, when you are inexperienced, like I was in 2014, sometimes you're a bitch about things. As a poet said: "A little knowledge is a dangerous thing."

Now, a year later, I happened to pick up the sample hoodie, probably out of the hallway to the back door, where odds and ends tended to get stacked . . . and it was fantastic. The fit was great. The cloth was high quality. The stitching was exact. What had I not liked about it?

So I called Grace to discuss a small order. She remembered me. She was easy to work with. She was accommodating, offering samples before I asked. Her prices were low but reasonable, not the kind that seem too good to be true. (They usually are.) You can tell when someone wants your business, and Grace wanted Cheekys.

I asked for pictures of her factory. I always ask before placing an order, and I study the facilities on Google Earth, too. Grace happily obliged. She took the photos right then, on her phone, and texted them to me. Her factory was small. It was outside a small town. Her machines weren't fancy or new. In fact, her presses used wooden, hand-operated panels.

Thank goodness we're not printing with them, I thought. Justin's presses were far more advanced than Grace's.

What impressed me about Grace's photos and descriptions,

though, was her pride. She loved this factory. She was proud of those old machines and the people working them. She cared about the products they made. This wasn't a wealthy company. They weren't working with big customers, and they clearly hadn't been started by millionaire investors. This was a local factory run by hardworking, ordinary people, in a rural part of China. When I looked at Grace and her factory, they reminded me of Cheekys.

I gave them a small order. They came through. So I gave them a larger order. Within six months, because my wholesale and Internet sales were growing so fast, I was buying out the custom hand-dyed shirts Grace's factory printed in bulk and kept in stock. So I started creating my own exclusive colors. You will not find Cheekys blue (or green or pink) on shirts from any other company.

Then I added the "butt tag," an extra tag at the back bottom of each shirt. I call them my "fortune cookies," because they have sayings like, "Butter my biscuits," or "I look just as good on the floor." I had about a hundred (because I love coming up with them), a challenge since factories like every piece in an order to be the same. Grace never complained. She figured out a way to mix and attach the labels so the sayings weren't all the same when she shipped a new batch of shirts. The Chicks went crazy for them. They write me all the time: "I love those little tags. I always look to see what I got first thing. That little message brightens my day."

I don't sell Cheekys merchandise on Amazon or any other big retail site. I don't sell to the large national chains, and I don't license my designs to third parties. You can only buy Cheekys items and Cheekys original designs from my website, my store, and boutiques that I approve of and that purchase directly from me.

Yes, I get knocked off. You can buy things that are *almost* Cheekys on Amazon and in stores like Wish. But the material and stitching will never be as high-quality as mine, because Grace custom stitches for me. The designs and colors will never be as good as my originals. And it won't have the little touches like "butt tags" that let you know Cheekys cares, and we want you to feel good every time you wear our clothes.

That happens because we buy the best and pay attention to every detail. It also happens because Grace puts in the extra time and effort to make those special details possible, at a reasonable price.

She keeps inviting me to China. She wants me to stay with her so she can show me her little corner of the world. I haven't done that, and I probably never will. I have allergies; it's a long way; I've never left America, except one time when my baby sister and I road-tripped eleven hours to cross the Idaho border into Canada, just to say we did. (It looked exactly like Idaho.) So Grace sends me photos and videos of the beautiful light parade her town holds every year. She emails me just to chat, and she gives me the best Christmas presents. One year, it was a hand-printed scroll. This year, it was a hand-stitched panda in a glass box.

I wouldn't say we're friends. We're partners who care deeply about the products and each other. She tells me all the time I'm her number one customer, and whether that is true or not I don't particularly care, because Grace sounds like she means it. She treats me the way I try to treat my employees, wholesalers, and customers: with respect, honesty, and personal attention.

That's what you want in business. Heck, that's what you want in life. When you find it, don't let it go. (I'm looking at you, Justin Roberts. Put down that red beer and give me a kiss, Mr. Furry Bottoms, because I'm never letting you go.)

In 2017, an India-based apparel manufacturer approached me with an offer I couldn't refuse: blank shirts for half the price I was paying, if I bought in bulk.

I should have known the offer was too good to be true, but I took it. I was greedy, y'all. He sent me samples that weren't right. His first templates had the wrong measurements. I *still* kept the order. Everything was telling me this was wrong, but I wanted 60,000 shirts at a super cheap price. This was how the Big Boys did it, right? This was "the next step."

The shirts arrived and, of course, they were a mess. Non-standard sizes, bad stitching, poor material, missing tags. Not to mention, they were eight months late. I called my contact. I said I wanted my money back. He was like, "Nope, tough break." He knew I would never do business with him again, so what did he care? I had to eat the whole order because I would never sell those crap shirts to my customers. It was a $160,000 loss.

One hundred sixty thousand dollars!

(continued)

A few months ago, I called Grace with a problem: some stitching on an order of shirts was black when I asked for green. She got back to me within an hour: "I am sorry, Jessi," she said. "I am giving you a six-hundred-dollar discount on your next order."

That didn't feel right, either. Six hundred dollars is a lot of money, especially for a stitch. The usual credit was more like sixty dollars. So I called her the next day. "Grace," I said, "are you taking this discount out of your own paycheck?"

"Yes," she said. "You're an important customer, and I must remind myself to pay careful attention to your orders."

I think I laughed. I said, "Grace, do not give me that much discount. I mean it. You don't need to punish yourself. You always treat me well."

Erica, my new lead designer, overheard the call. When I hung up, she said, "Too bad we don't get a discount like that from our jewelry guy. He's always screwing up."

My jewelry guy is so important to my business that I won't even give you his first name. And I'm important to his business, too. He told me after six months I was his biggest customer. He told me a year later I was the biggest customer the company had ever had in its twenty-five years in business. He has come here, to New Plymouth, to work on jewelry designs with me. That's how tight we are.

"What do you mean?" I said, surprised Erica had anything to complain about. "He credits us for mistakes, right?"

"Of course, but he never pays for it out of his pocket."

I said, "Erica, he owns the company. Every time he gives us a credit or discount, it comes out of his pocket." *And every time you make a mistake, it comes out of mine.*

She just looked at me for a second, then smiled. "Yeah," she said. "I guess I didn't think that through, did I?"

CHAPTER 14

THE CHICKEN AND THE EGG

One of the most important concepts in the retail business is space. You are always working within a space, and no matter how large or small that space is, you have to fill it. From day one, I had to buy enough merchandise to fill my store. I had to provide content to fill and update my Facebook page. As a wholesaler, I needed a full line for customers to browse. To me, that meant a *minimum* of twenty-four designs, in a variety of colors and materials, with a new design at least every ten days. It was a tremendous amount of work, and by 2015 it was pushing up against even my workaholic tendencies. You only have a certain amount of space (time plus energy) in your life, especially as a mom, and you have to think carefully about how you use it.

And the more I thought, the more I realized I had a big fundamental business question sitting there staring me in the face: Was Cheekys a store or a brand?

Up to then, we were a store. Everything about my Facebook page, my marketing, and my operation was designed around the idea that I was a small retail outlet on a little main street in rural Idaho. My other business lines simply translated what I did in New Plymouth to the wholesaling and electronic space.

But was that Cheekys anymore?

Or, more important, was that what I wanted Cheekys to be in the future?

Because there was another way to think about the company: that Cheekys was a clothing and accessories line designed and partially manufactured in New Plymouth, and that it reflected and embodied our small-town Idaho lifestyle, but was sold everywhere. In that view, the store wasn't the center of the Cheekys universe. It was simply one store among the many boutiques carrying our merchandise. A special one, sure, because it was first, and because I put my heart and soul into it, but still *a client* of the main Cheekys business, which was design and manufacture.

Do you see the difference? It's fundamental, but subtle. What came first, the chicken or the egg? The egg! (The store. The compact space that incubated the idea.) But what was more important? It felt more and more like the answer was the chicken, and that I should be feeding and grooming and caring for that.

Now, I loved my physical store. Justin built me a dream space, and I spent four years filling it with extra touches—free cards with cute sayings, old-fashioned bulbs in metal chandeliers, silo-style dressing rooms. I did my photo shoots there; I held events; I sold women all over the world on the fact that Cheekys wasn't just a style or an attitude, it was a place: a small store in a small town with a big, caring heart.

That was real, because my love for New Plymouth was real. I

loved the wide main street and the hundred-year-old Western architecture. I loved that on some nights, without warning, The Club would fill up with cowboys in from the ranches. I loved that my children could ride their foot scooters down Plymouth Avenue to the Pilgrim Market without having to worry about traffic. I loved the mountains, and the rodeo, and the Big Nasty, the yearly motorcycle race up the steep dirt cliffs two miles outside town. I'll never get tired of smelling the fresh-cut mint where the highway exit dips out of the high plains into the Payette Valley and the farms spread out before me. That's the smell of home.

I gave everything I could to New Plymouth. When a coffee shop and lunch counter called The Rustic Cup opened across from Cheekys, I designed their logo and sign. That was a $5,000 job, but I only charged her a couple hundred dollars, because I knew the owner not only couldn't afford a graphic design company, she didn't even know how to find one.

I did that over and over. At one point, Cheekys had designed, below cost, new logos or signs for almost every business in town: The Club, the Double Diamond, the Pilgrim Market, the Eazy Mart, Ballistic Boats, Some Days Discount Grocery (since closed). We designed and manufactured shirts for local fundraisers; we organized raffles and contests; and since I was no longer too broke to feed my children, we gave to just about everyone who walked in the door. If a kid came in selling candy bars for the middle school band, my husband bought the whole box.

"Most people buy a bar, Justin," I said. "You just bought twenty-six!"

"It's a good cause, Jessi, what could I do? Why don't we just give them away to customers in the store."

We didn't do any of that for the giveback. We didn't do it for public relations. We did it because we loved New Plymouth. It's who we are.

But New Plymouth didn't love us back in the same way. People were thankful, but they never understood how much money and work it was to design their logos and print their shirts. Some of the more successful men considered a women's store a joke. They laughed among themselves and referred to Cheekys as "the little corner junk shop," because they had no idea the kind of business I was doing online and no desire to find out. Some of the women still talked behind my back, especially now that I had a new lawyer and was trying to regain primary custody of Sterling and Jack. The local Kiwanis Club made a calendar. Every business in town was featured, down to the high school girls who babysat on the weekend. Cheekys wasn't asked to participate. Everybody in town's birthday was supposed to be on the calendar. Nobody from my family was included, except Justin, and his birthday was listed on the wrong day.

It sounds small, I know. It is small, especially the calendar, but it got to me. *I was the only freaking retail store in the downtown!* There was no way those people accidently missed me.

There were more serious problems, too, especially for Hunter. The boy tried, I can tell you that. He was active in 4-H. He played on the school football team, even though he didn't like sports, and he wasn't any good. But he's a unique kid, with a unique style. He wears a big gold chain. He collects funky sneakers and colorful jackets. He gels his hair, but not country, more like Brooklyn. (I assume—I've never been to Brooklyn.) He *idolizes* Kanye West, for his fashion and attitude as much as his music. When Morgan's boyfriend dumped her two days before senior prom, Hunter stepped in. She was a senior, he was a freshman, and he had a big crush on her. He worked hard on his outfit. He wanted to wear high-top Supra sneakers with a white tux, so he took Morgan to a store in Ontario, explained his idea, and bought her a pair of Supras. Morgan was an ag girl. To her, casual meant boots, but she went along with it, because I don't think any boy had ever talked to her and bought things for her and respected her like Hunter. The prom pictures of them in white high-tops with purple laces to match Morgan's purple dress are beyond adorable.

People—adults!—were offended. They didn't see a careful, thoughtful kid. All they saw were weird shoes.

Hunter can be a smartass. Believe me, I live with him, I know. He has ADHD. He's not a diligent student. The only book I'll probably ever convince him to read is this one, because he's in it. But Hunter wasn't a bad kid, with an emphasis on *kid*. It's tough to be the odd one out. His attitude and style were his way of taking control of his life.

But some teachers and school administrators in New Plymouth didn't like him, and they weren't shy about saying it. They called him worthless, an idiot, and worse. They let him know he didn't matter, and that they'd laugh when he ended up in jail, they'd enjoy it so much. And Hunter was pretty much a normal kid, if you judge by the whole country, not just rural Idaho!

In seventh grade, Hunter brought a pocketknife to school. It was an accident. He was up at dawn cutting the twine on a hay bale to feed our calves, and he stuck the knife in his back pocket. We're a farm community; that's fairly common. Well, a teacher saw him show the knife to a friend at lunch, and the principal *had him hauled out by the police in handcuffs*. They charged him with felony counts of possessing a weapon and assault with a deadly weapon . . . for a four-inch Browning pocketknife that never touched or threatened anyone.

The sheriff was laughing when I rushed down to the station. "It's nothing," he said. "I'm just gonna shake him up a bit and let him go. I do it with kids all the time."

"It's a big deal," I said, and I wasn't talking about the principal's overreaction. This was in the middle of my custody dispute. "You're going to get a call. They're going to make this out to be the crime of the century."

"Nah," the sheriff said. "Nobody'll even know."

They introduced Hunter to a mock parole officer and prosecuting attorney. They had a whole system set up for this kind of thing. It was kind of a joke to them . . . until the "parole officer" was called out of his office with Hunter and me standing right there. He came back a few minutes later looking like he'd seen a ghost.

"That was them, wasn't it?" It had been maybe half an hour. They clearly had someone in the school to tip them off.

"Yeah, it was . . . And you were right. They're going to war."

"Well," I said, desperate for help, "don't you think there's a connection between that and the way my son is being treated?"

I mean, it seemed obvious to me that Hunter was being singled out because of the harassing accusations against me and my family.

It only got worse for him after that. Someone stole the school bus, took it for a joyride, and crashed it. The first house the police and high school principal came to was ours. Thank God Hunter was with his father in Texas.

A year later, someone came up to me on the street. "I saw your son smoking cigarettes behind the Pilgrim Market," he said, smirking.

"Oh, yeah, when was that?"

"Last night."

"Well, Hunter's been in Texas with his dad for the last two weeks."

You should have seen the look on his face. The man was *crushed.* What kind of adult has it in for a child like that? Hunter doesn't smoke. He doesn't drink. He doesn't use drugs. He's a straight-edge kid with a cocky attitude and a ridiculous wardrobe. But because of his family—because of me—some people wanted to put bad things on him.

It came to a head in the spring of 2015, with the poetry project. Everyone in Hunter's class had to choose a theme and write thirty poems about it. Hunter chose death. His English teacher was not pleased. (Neither was I. *Really, son? Help me out here.*) She called me and ripped the shit out of my son for choosing that theme. Mommin' ain't for the faint of heart, y'all.

So I went to Hunter, and I said, "I don't know why you chose that theme, Hunter. You're not Goth, or obsessed with death, or whatever. But I'm going to challenge you to really think about this subject, and to really put your heart and soul into this project. I know you're capable of incredible work. Show these people what you can do."

He said, "Okay, mom, I will."

Hunter worked so hard on that project. He talked about his ideas with me every night, and we discussed each poem. Honestly, it was one of the best months we'd had together since moving to New Plymouth. He expanded the project to include not just literal death, but metaphorical death, too. He wrote a poem about the death of his relationship with his father. He wrote about losing a father figure when Ben's dad, Charlie, died. He had to design a poem in the shape of an object. He wrote about the death of a violent childhood, and he made the poem into a gun. That poem was about my life. Hunter knew some of what I had endured growing up, although he didn't know most.

I read every poem—Hunter was so into the project, he wrote more than the required thirty—and I was filled with wonder. I said, "Hunter, this is beautiful."

He said, "Thanks, mom," with his sideways smile, like I was being a total dork. But I could tell he was proud of himself.

Two days after he turned in the project, he called me from school. His voice was cracking. "Mom," he said, "you need to get down here right now."

He was in the office with the principal, one of the biggest assholes I've ever met, and I was raised by real dogshits. "We need to talk about this poetry project," the principal said.

"Okay. What grade did Hunter get?"

"We gave him a sixty-nine." One point below passing. Classy.

"Why?" I was pissed. And my son was crying.

The principal did a tough-guy mug. "This project has all the warning signs of a school shooter."

Bullshit. "Did you read these poems?" I asked.

"I looked at them. There's one in here about a drive-by."

"Well, I read every word of these poems. I gave Hunter advice on these poems. The poem you're referring to is about my childhood. It's not a threat. That really happened in my life."

I could tell he was shocked. He didn't expect me to have carefully read and discussed his work with Hunter. But a bully never backs down. "Well," he said, "I've been talking to Hunter. I don't think this is the right school for him. I think he needs to attend the alternative high school."

Hold on. Hold the f*ck on. Number one, you're kicking my son out of a public school? And number two, you talked to him about it, *and threatened him*, before you talked to me? I don't think so.

I said, "Hunter's coming home with me. But he's coming back tomorrow. You are not driving my son out of this school."

But what was I fighting for? People in town had been treating Hunter like that for years. We had been gossiped about since the moment we stepped foot in New Plymouth. It just started to feel like, when it came down to it, nobody really wanted us here.

So I sold out.

I quit.

Not Cheekys. I kept the Cheekys brand. But I sold the store. The idea had started forming when a woman emailed me for advice on opening a boutique in Mountain Home, a small town two hours away in eastern Idaho. I invited her to New Plymouth to study what I'd done. She showed up with her baby and her husband, an old-school rancher in boots, a pearl-button shirt, and a cowboy hat. He didn't say a word the whole tour, until the end, when he said, standing in the middle of my store with the baby on his hip: "Well, shoot, honey, why reinvent the wheel? Why not just copy this?"

Typical rancher. Straight to the point.

So I licensed her the Cheekys name, and we worked out a profit-sharing deal for Cheekys merchandise. I spent a week in Mountain Home advising her on locations, costs, and brand marketing. Then Justin tore down our second-to-last barn and built her a beautiful store. It took a month of twelve-hour days, but that's Justin, he'll never half-ass the first 98 percent of a building project! He installed shiplap wooden walls, homemade metal light fixtures, and a funky old-fashioned sign. It probably cost me $20,000, because I didn't want to gouge her or put her into debt, but after that initial investment all I had to do was fill her orders and cash her licensing checks.

If it can work like that, I thought, *why do I need to own any stores?*

Look, this wasn't defeat. I had succeeded, wildly and beyond my own initial hopes. I had turned my "little corner junk shop" into a multi-million-dollar business. I had created a Facebook community of 50,000 Cheekys Chicks, many of whom regularly participated in discussions and posted comments. I had Cheekys Chicks living in every town for fifty miles, and every time we unloaded our trailer at an event, we had local fans. Cheekys was at every rodeo on the Idaho circuit that year—except the one in New Plymouth. New Plymouth gave an exclusive to a boutique owner from Nampa because her husband supplied the bulls, so I was banned in my own hometown.

But what did that matter? Cheekys wasn't a store. It wasn't dependent on the good people of New Plymouth, Idaho. It was a brand.

So I approached one woman, privately, to see if she wanted to buy the store. She was a super-fan from out of state who for years had bought more merchandise than anyone else. She was one of the first Chicks to regularly post comments to our Face-book page, and she often called and chatted with us (something we can no longer do, sorry). She'd say, "I want to buy everything in the store, Jessi. How much would that cost?"

I knew she wanted, more than anything, to be part of Cheekys. So I said, "I can't sell you everything in the store... but I can sell you the store itself."

She was in her fifties. She had thirty years in with the Department of Agriculture, so she was eligible for early retire-ment. *Who could be more perfect?* She had experience, free time, a solid pension, and a genuine passion for the brand. And most important, she could afford it.

So I sold her my Cheekys store for a below-market price. I thought I was so smart. I had traded a commitment I'd out-grown for two things I really needed: the time and money to grow Cheekys into a national brand.

It was an absolute, total, complete disaster. Within a month, I realized she had no idea how to run a store. She kept irregular hours. She treated customers like...customers. She didn't market or give to local charity and, worst of all, she didn't restock. I had rented the former post office behind the store for my wholesale, Internet, and design operations. We were literally five feet away; we shared a wall, but not a door. Yet she never bought more Cheekys merchandise to replace what she sold.

The problem was clear: This woman liked the *idea* of owning a Cheekys store, but she had no interest in doing the hard work to run one. And believe me, it's hard work. Owning a store is not a hobby. It's a full-time job. If you just want to own a big closet, you're not going to succeed.

It took about sixty days for the paychecks to start bouncing. Miranda and Dana were long-time Cheekys employees, and they had stuck with the store. At that point, their experience and hard work were the only things keeping it from collapse. So I paid them every penny they were owed out of my pocket, even though they no longer worked for me, because nobody stiffs my girls. It didn't help. The new owner's behavior only became more erratic. One day, she came in with a full gallon of ice cream, sat down at the counter, and ate it while crying. I felt both pity and disgust, but there was nothing more I could do to help her. She was going down, and she was taking the store with her. So I invoked a clause in the contract terminating her license.

By then, things were falling apart in Mountain Home. Let's just say, because she has a family to feed and a life to succeed at, too, the owner was cutting too many corners, and Justin and I found out. I said, "You know I have to take away your license, right?"

"Yeah," she said, looking down. "I know." She didn't argue. She knew what she'd been doing wasn't right.

I remembered that straight-shooting rancher, with their daughter on his hip. Men like that were honest before anything. "What does your husband think?"

"He's disappointed in me," she said, and I could tell that hurt.

"Good. If you remember that feeling, you won't make these mistakes again."

It was good advice for me, too, because I walked out of that meeting feeling about as bad as I'd ever felt over Cheekys. *What have you done, Jessi?* I thought. *What have you done to the business you love?*

And how the heck are you going to fix it?

CHAPTER 15

CHOOSE JOY

You may realize by now that Daddy Joe, my father's father, was one of the heroes of my life. And you may remember that after God struck down the 1980s Texas oil boom because of Daddy Joe's extravagance in taking his wife on a vacation to Spain, the man decided to give every extra penny he earned for the rest of his life to those in need. And people loved him for it. When he died in 2004, they shut three plumbing companies for the day to honor him, because Daddy Joe was a plumber, and he'd helped or hired just about every plumber in the Permian Basin in one way or another. His funeral was held in the gym he'd paid to build at his beloved church, and it overflowed that giant space, because more than 2,000 people came to pay him respect.

Afterward, the close family drove his body four hours to his isolated property way up in the Fort Davis Mountains, where there were no paved roads, no cell service, and hardly any signs of human habitation. We dug his grave by hand behind the lit-tle one-room church where he worshipped, then held a private service with a minister who drove the four hours from Midland with the rest of us. I sang "Amazing Grace" as we stood over his grave, and then the seven of us who were closest to him stayed for the rest of the day, processing our grief as we slowly filled in the hole, the sun setting over us and then finally disappearing behind the edge of that barren, rocky ground.

One of the things Daddy Joe believed in most, other than God, humility, and always doing everything the right way, was Pathways, the Christian self-help program founded by Dr. Phil McGraw long before Oprah made him famous. Daddy Joe was a hard man. They called him "Judge Roy Bean" in the program, because it was impossible to get him to compliment, comfort, or even smile. But after Pathways, he went to every member of the family, sat down with them, and said he loved them. That change was so profound for him that over the years he paid to send more than a hundred people through Pathways. He sent me twice, once at fifteen, and once at twenty-two, after my divorce from Ben. It didn't straighten me all the way out—I was too messed up back then—but it taught me that W didn't own me, and that I could *Be Pretty* without being hurt. In fact, my first contract with myself was: "I can be pretty without being a victim of other people's actions." It's still something I remind myself of every day.

I enrolled in Pathways again in 2015, during the summer I was losing the store and challenging Nick and his mother for custody of the boys. Justin was supposed to attend with me, but when we got to Texas he bailed to work with my ex-husband (and his good friend) Ben. So Hunter went with me into the program, even though he wasn't any more enthusiastic about it than Justin. He was only seventeen, so he had no choice. He was still legally required to obey his mom.

I hated it. I had such happy memories of that place. It had changed my life. But this time I hated the counselors; I hated the phrases and dialogues; and I especially hated a woman in my group named Kaci. Pathways is an expensive program, so it was mostly respectable Christian professionals from the suburbs. Kaci, though, was a mess: she had lost her husband, she had lost her kids, she had big tattoos on her neck and who knows where else, and she had no job. She was "in school," she kept saying in a loud voice, even though she was almost forty like me, and she wouldn't shut up about it. Finally, after two days, I let loose on her in a group session. I said, "I'm tired of you, Kaci. I'm tired of your attitude, and I'm tired of your confidence. It's trashy women like you that cause people to look down on women like me who lose their kids, even though I was a good mom, and I'm a good person, and I didn't deserve it."

She just looked at me and smiled. She said, "Okay, Jessi. I hear you. I understand."

It made me hate her even more. I thought, *Why are you being so nice to me, when I'm being such a bitch to you?*

I found out her story the next day. She had been married to a soldier, and he stole their two children in the middle of the night and disappeared. She quit her job and moved to Dallas to look for them. The big tattoo on her forearm was a medical alert, because she'd given a kidney to save a stranger and the EMTs needed to know that if she was in an accident. The big tattoo on

her neck was the names of her children. She'd had it put there
so they would know, even if she died, and they only saw pictures
of her, that she had always loved them. She wasn't a bad person.
Not at all. In fact, Kaci was an awesome person and an awesome
mom. And I had judged her without knowing her, the same way
I felt all those people in New Plymouth had judged me.

That realization didn't make Pathways any better. In fact, all
it did was fill me with more anger and shame, and I was already
full of those things. They call people who fight the program
"desperados," and I was the desperado's desperado that summer. I fought everything anybody said to me. The program was
bringing up so much from inside me—so much pain and shame
and confusion and fear—that I didn't know what else to do.

Eventually, they'd had enough. They said, "We don't usually
do this, Jessi, but your son has something to say to you, and we
think you should hear it."

They brought Hunter into the adult training room. He didn't
want to be there, I could see that, but he gathered himself, took
a deep breath, and said, "Mom, they're kicking us out. They say
you're not participating and causing problems."

"Fine," I said. "Let's leave. They don't understand me here,
and we don't need this."

"No, mom," Hunter said, "I need you to stay, because I need
you to change." He paused, but he didn't look away. "I need you
to be happy."

I was stunned. "Hunter," I snapped, "I don't know if I can be
happy. I am heartbroken."

Hunter said, "This isn't a request, mom. Addy and I need our mother back."

We were in a room full of people, but right then, for a moment, it was only Hunter and me, *and I saw him.* I saw my son for the sensitive and intelligent young man he is, and I saw the hurt I'd put on him. I saw that, in the only way that mattered, I was failing him. All I ever wanted in life was to give my children happy memories. I never had those. I wanted their lives to be different. I wanted them to know joy.

But I was failing at that, and it was so clear, suddenly, that even I could see it. I had lost my way when I lost the twins. It had been two years, and I still cried myself to sleep every night. I still stared into their empty rooms for hours. We stopped going on family getaways, because I thought, *We can't go camping without Jack and Sterling; they'll feel left out.* I stopped taking Hunter and Addy shopping, because I thought it wasn't fair, giving to them but not their brothers. We never ate steak anymore, because I thought, *How can we eat something nice, and enjoy it, when we're not doing it as a family?*

Even Nick said once, when I broke down dropping off the twins at his house, "I never thought this would affect you so much." He wasn't nasty, either. I think he was shocked.

But my unhappiness went deeper than losing the boys. It went back through my whole life. I had so much to be thankful for—Justin, my children, my business, my friends, my Chicks, my dad, who was fighting cancer but more alive in Idaho than he'd been in a long, long time. I had made it out of abuse, neglect, and bad relationships. I built a life on my own, and then I found a man I loved to partner with. I had my perfect four acres and my imperfect but wonderful little town. I had my special place on Earth, where I could build the life I wanted, *and I built that life*. I built it. I won. And yet, all this time, I'd been pushing it away.

Because I was afraid. Because deep down, I lived in fear. Of losing everything. Of being found out. Of not measuring up. Of being nothing more than a grown-up version of that little girl in that abandoned house whom nobody loved. And that fear, that sadness and anxiety, was hurting the people I loved.

"I'm sorry," I said, through tears I didn't know I had been crying. "I am so sorry, Hunter. I want to change. I want to be happy. I really do. But I don't know how."

He said, "Happiness isn't a skill, mom. It's a choice."

I can't say everything changed after that. Life is like a business: Success isn't about one breakthrough, it's about taking a small step forward every day. But some steps are more important than others, and that moment with Hunter was one of the most important of my life.

I acknowledged my feelings of inadequacy. I took control. I started appreciating where I was and what I had. I stopped dwelling, as much as I could, on my hurt and frustration. I let Addy and Hunter tell me what they needed, and I listened. I started cooking steaks again, and they were freaking delicious. I missed steaks so much. We squeezed in small family trips.

I let Hunter transfer to Payette High School for his senior year like he wanted. I couldn't believe the parent-teacher conferences. Every teacher said, "Hunter is such a good student. He has a great personality. I love having him in my class."

Are you serious?!

Hunter is a talented graphic artist, so one of his teachers, Mr. Bingham, convinced the school administration to buy some design software. One day, the district supervisors were touring the school, and one stopped to ask Hunter what he was doing. Hunter spent twenty minutes showing him how the software worked and what he had created with it. The man put his hand on Hunter's shoulder and said, "I'm going to remember your name, son, because you are going to do great things."

"That's the first time anyone at school said they would remember me," Hunter told me proudly that night. "Well, without saying it was because I would end up in jail."

That made me feel so good...but also sort of terrible. Why had I left my son in that environment so long? Why hadn't I understood what was happening to him? I guess I never realized how bad it was. Or more likely, how good it could be.

By then, the custody case had made it back to court, so the state assigned another evaluator. He sat me down. He said, "This is the most contentious case I've ever worked on, and that's not healthy for the boys. So let me ask you: Is this about winning, Jessi, or is it about what's best for your sons?"

He was right. It hurt, but he was right. I was wounded, and I was angry, so I had to take some blame for how rotten things had become with Nick. My love for Jack and Sterling, and even my sadness over losing them, had tipped over into selfishness, and thanks to Hunter, I could see and accept that fact. For all our disagreements, I believe Nick had grown to love the boys deeply. Neither of us would ever intentionally hurt them.

"I want what's best for them," I said. *I want them to have good memories of their childhood.*

"Then trust me," he said, "and accept what I decide."

I trusted him, so I agreed. He gave Nick and me joint custody, with a complicated schedule called a snake to minimize the disruptions in the boys' lives. And I have to admit: I miss Jack and Sterling when they aren't with me, but it's fair. It's the best for them.

Soon after, in fall 2015, I closed the Cheekys store. It was devastating. I never would have done it if I had any other choice, but the contractual terms for regaining control placed a two-year restriction on me owning or licensing *any* retail space in New Plymouth.

I didn't want another store, not if it couldn't be in New Plymouth. But one of my hair stylists, Kristie, wanted to open a Cheekys in Fruitland. I was skeptical. I mean, look what just happened when I licensed the store!

But I knew Kristie. She worked hard. She was smart. She came to my house and barbequed with my family. She was a single mom, dedicated to her two young boys. And she had financing. So two months after I closed the New Plymouth Cheekys, Kristie opened the new "new" Cheekys retail store six miles away in a former Subway sandwich shop on the busiest intersection in Fruitland, Idaho.

I never told anyone about the contractual obligations that forced me out of New Plymouth. I never told anyone I had sold the store or that Kristie owned the new one. I let them assume I had simply outgrown my old space. Then I frosted the big glass window on Plymouth Avenue and turned my old location into a warehouse and shipping center for my exploding wholesale and Internet business.

It felt like I'd turned my back on my town. And that felt like I'd betrayed something important, because I loved New Plymouth. I could feel that love in my bones, in a way I hadn't before. I loved *that store* in *that location* in New Plymouth. I loved the women who had shopped there, and I loved being part of a real, working rural community. I was still in the space, but my lights were no longer shining on our downtown strip. My front door was no longer open, only the back. So my neighbors never stopped in to chat any more. The local charities never came to ask for help. Nobody came from other towns to shop or get their hair styled. When The Rustic Cup went out of business, I felt partially responsible.

"She really struggled after Cheekys left," someone posted on Facebook. She wasn't angry. She was resigned. *This is how it is. This is how it's always been.*

Looking back, I don't think New Plymouth ostracized me on purpose. I mean, some people, sure, but that's true no matter where you live. Popular people will shun us regular girls. Older men will be sexist jerks when they see a woman trying to better herself. Haters gonna hate, that's Proverbs 9:8, and who am I to question God's truth?

But most people in New Plymouth were good to us. They appreciated having Cheekys in town. The calendar thing?

Probably an accident. The lack of appreciation? That was just rural reticence. Nobody gives you a gold star out here for getting through the day. Nobody gives you a gold star for helping them through their day. At best, you get a tip of the cowboy hat, and a "thank ya," before they head out onto the range. And that's from the women. The men are even more reserved.

If anything, I suspect the town was scared to embrace us. Every place like Cheekys in New Plymouth had gone out of a business or moved on over the last forty years. Every one. I think, deep down, they always figured I'd skip out, too. After all, I wasn't from New Plymouth, and that's what out-of-towners did.

And guess what? They were right. That's what I did.

In the end, I can see now, the frustration and anger I sometimes felt toward New Plymouth wasn't a window onto the town's soul, like I convinced myself at my lowest moments. It was a mirror, looking back on mine.

That's a lesson, y'all. It's one I'm trying to live every day. It's simple, but it will help take your business, your family, your life, your everything where you want them to be.

When you have a chance to speak, *choose kindness.*

When you have a chance to teach, *choose openheartedness.*

When you have a chance to react, *choose joy.*

CHAPTER 16

GROWING UP AND BUILDING OUT:

A SUCCESSFUL GIRL'S GUIDE TO MARKETING

So Cheekys was now an Internet business. I didn't have a store in New Plymouth. I had a headquarters in New Plymouth and a store on Facebook. That meant, of course, I needed to be smart and knowledgeable about what was happening online.

When I put Cheekys on Facebook in 2011, the site didn't cater to small businesses. The first marketing tool I remember was an offer to mention your business in their general feed and encourage users to become fans of your page. (Back then, it was "fans," then "followers," now it's "like." Tomorrow? Who knows?)

That didn't make sense to me. I wanted customers, not fans. I wasn't a celebrity; I was a shop owner. "Fans" weren't going to feed my kids. And besides, I couldn't afford it. So I kept growing the hard way, by posting frequently and treating everyone who came to my page like a queen.

Other boutiques took Facebook up on their offer. Some blew up overnight to 500,000 or even a million fans. They used that number to secure bank loans while Cheekys, with its 900 followers, was turned down. Those "fans" weren't loyal, though. They were just people checking a box. When Facebook changed its algorithm, they disappeared. That's not a bug in their system; it's a feature. Facebook is a thresher. They change their algorithm *for the express purpose of weeding out companies that game their system*, and whenever they do, they destroy hundreds of honest, small, and often small-town businesses that rely on the audience they built on the platform. I know boutique owners whose sales dropped 50 percent in a week. I know a woman who lost 90 percent of her business overnight. *You cannot rely on Facebook or on social media promotions that promise to multiply your followers or trick people into giving you information.* Be active in your marketing. Most boutique owners who used Facebook's "fans" program were left with nothing but crushing debt.

Then Facebook started placing small ads within their feed. I was on the platform four hours a day, updating my page and interacting with the Chicks, so I noticed them. And if I noticed them, I figured other people did, too. I was at maybe 2,000 followers, making a little money, so I decided to try it.

I thought: *What would I want to see from a company like Cheekys?*

The answer was easy: real women, in real places, wearing real clothes.

I didn't want people to think, "Oh, look, an ad." I wanted their first thought to be, "Wait, do I know her?"

So in 2013, I started spending a hundred dollars a month on simple ads with our logo and a photo of a Chick (or Chicks) wearing our clothes. The models were employees and friends, often Miranda, because she has a beautiful, approachable look, but I had also, for a long time, been encouraging customers to send pictures of themselves in their favorite outfits. If you look at our history, you'll see hundreds of ordinary women in Cheekys items. Those photos really capture what Cheekys is about, so I started using some in ads, with permission. It doesn't get more real, after all, than the smile on a woman's face when she loves her new top.

The ads worked. Instead of a hundred new followers a week, we were getting 300 or more. We were also attracting trolls. Facebook was sending the ads to random accounts, so I'd get angry responses like: "I saw guns on your shirts. Guns kill, asshole."

Or: "Ignorant rural people like you are ruining this country."

We had a lot of complaints about the word "gypsy." It's funny: Almost no one complains about "bullshit," but people flip out over "gypsy." Now, I know way back the phrase was a slur against the Romani people, but that's not how it's used today. Today, a gypsy means a free thinker, a free wheeler, a woman who refuses to be tied down. What the heck is negative about that?

After a while I said, "Forget it. Forget the ads. Too much trouble."

Our most effective marketing tool was the auction site, anyway. It was a closed group accessible only to people approved by us, so it was a safe place for women (and men) who loved country life, fast fashion, sassy talk—and yes, guns, and alcohol in moderation. And it was an encouraging place for women who didn't feel comfortable with themselves because of their job, their weight, their neighborhood, or that spouse who never treated them like they were special and loved. We *always* treated them like they were special and loved. Nobody sent a photo without hearing back from us and their fellow group members: "You wear it, girl!" or "Looking good, girl!" Or 🖤🖤🖤🖤🖤

By 2015, Facebook had refined its advertising system. Now you could target with criteria like: female only, America only, follows Cabela's. My ads would only go to that smaller group, but it might hit them every day for a week. Targeting was perfect for a company like Cheekys, because we have a niche. Ninety-five percent of Americans have never heard of us, and I couldn't care less. It's like that old Sawyer Brown song, "Some Girls Do." *I ain't first class, but I ain't white trash. Not all girls like me, but some girls do.* I'm in it for those girls.

With the ability to target, I upped my advertising budget to $400 a month. That was terrifying. I figured Justin would kill me when he found out. It's one thing to pay $400 a month for a tractor...

No, $400 a month won't even rent a mini-tractor, but it will buy a truckload of lumber, and that's something Justin understood: $400 for wood, $400 the next month for pipe, and pretty soon you have 98 percent of a Hen Den in your backyard. Four hundred dollars for shirts, and you have a tall stack of merchandise. But $400 for advertising just seemed to disappear.

I had to think of that money as rent. I ran a store. You can't have a store without paying for a location where customers can find you. My online store was free, but it was also invisible to anybody not looking for it, so I had to pay my rent in the form of advertising. My ad budget wasn't about justifying an extra expense. It was about figuring out the "location" I wanted. Main Street? Back street? Shopping mall? When I started thinking of it that way, I realized $400 a month—or even $1,000 a month—was a bargain. (At one point, after Cheekys took off, I was spending $4,000 a week. I don't do that anymore.)

I didn't just throw out the money and hope the ads worked. I studied the results. Everyone counts new followers; I visited their Facebook pages to find out who they were. I didn't want too many negative people, the kind whose pages were filled with cursing and conspiracy theories and hatred toward their mother-in-law. I also didn't want too many Barbie dolls. I have nothing against those women, with their blown blond hair, posed photos, and tight body dresses. I love my rodeo queens. But they aren't our primary audience. If the results started to skew too far either way, I knew I needed to adjust my ad criteria.

I learned even more from the new women in our target audience. Their Facebook photos and profiles gave me critical information like: What activities did they like? What other stores did they shop at? What musicians and television shows did they follow? What products did they love? I don't make coolers, but if I saw Yeti coolers in the background of enough photos, I knew to target followers of Yeti with my ads (which I do).

I studied their clothes, too. What patterns did they like? What material? What cut? I have picked up so many trends, and designed so many successful items, by studying what Chicks wear when they aren't wearing Cheekys. This company isn't about my style, after all. It's about *our* style.

Then Facebook introduced a blue check mark. A lot of boutiques were still buying followers, because plenty of companies promise software that manipulates the system. (Avoid those companies. Get your hands down in the mud.) I remember being butt-hurt because so many fly-by-night boutiques with fake followers were getting blue check marks, while Cheekys was turned down.

I didn't even know what a blue check mark was! My account rep at Facebook told me not to worry, but I freaking worried. If Filly Flair had a blue check mark, I wanted one, too! Turns out a blue check mark just meant your followers could be targeted with your business name in the Facebook ad system.

So did I target boutiques with that check mark? You bet I did!

It's a cutthroat business, girls, that's part of the game.

My goal wasn't to steal customers. I was a wholesaler, and the way to expand that business was to introduce myself to boutique owners. If those "blue check" stores watched their Facebook reports, they would see Cheekys targeting them. Hopefully, they would then go to my page, see what Cheekys was selling, and become a client. It worked, because I met a lot of strong, like-minded women that way. They are some of my smartest buyers.

The thing I liked best, though, was that none of my personal issues mattered online. Was I entangled with the New Plymouth school system? Was my custody situation gossip fodder in the Payette Valley? Who cares! Cheekys wasn't about me. I never talked about myself on our Facebook page. I never claimed this was my style, my genius, or my club. Back then, my picture wasn't even on our site. Cheekys was a group. It was all of us. The Chicks didn't think of me as the Boss Lady. They knew me as just another encouraging friend on their computer screen, and as long as I kept responding and caring and offering great merchandise, they were satisfied. And that's exactly how I wanted it.

But growth created other challenges. I now had two physical spaces to pay for: the warehouse in New Plymouth and the new store in Fruitland, because Kristie's financing had fallen apart and I ended up as her financial backer. Instead of buying a hundred blank shirts at a time, I was buying a thousand, and that meant thousands of dollars in up-front cost. Then Justin needed a fancy new printing press to keep up with demand, and even used at a bargain price, it was a $100,000 investment.

The thing was an octopus; it had metal arms everywhere. It was too large for the storage shed and, as we discovered after the purchase, too heavy for the floor of our space downtown. So we built out Justin's workshop and moved the printing operation to our backyard. Then we built a second entrance to our property for trucks and put a cargo container beside the gravel "parking pad" for Justin's tools. It was our first cargo container, but not our last. By 2017, we had six cargo containers outside the back door blocking my view of the mountains.

Even *all that* wasn't the end of the expenses, because the electrical system on our rural road wasn't strong or reliable enough to run the press. Cheekys had to pay to upgrade the power lines, then add a second electrical box at our property. We've been talking with the county about upgrading their

entire electrical and Wi-Fi systems for two years, and I think it's
going to happen. But that's another problem with being rural:
It's not just too many people stuck in the 1950s; it's too much
infrastructure stuck in the fifties, too.

Meanwhile, despite $2 million a year in sales, I couldn't get a
loan. A local bank gave a man a pile of money to open a Cross-
Fit in Fruitland, but with Cheekys it was: "Independent retailer.
Locally owned. Female focused. No savings?"

"We've been in business five years. We've grown our revenue
every quarter. Justin and I put the company first, before our personal comfort. This loan is for less than three months of revenue
at our current size, and we've been growing at twenty percent a
month for the past three years." *And we're right next door!*

"Sorry. Women are fickle about fashion. It's too risky."

PayPal kept us afloat. Their algorithm offered advances based
on the revenue you generated through their system. It started
at $5,000. If you paid that back within thirty days—based on
PayPal's share of payments, so a $5,000 payback meant about
$150,000 in total sales through their platform—you qualified
for another advance. I almost always cleared my advance within
ten days, so PayPal kept increasing my credit line. By 2016, I
was up to $50,000, enough to cover electrical issues, slow sales
weeks, and the up-front cost of large orders. Seriously, this service alone makes PayPal worth it, because independent, small-
town, blue-collar women are the last people banks want to work
with.

With that settled, it was time to take a step I'd been dreading
for years: staffing up.

I'd had employees forever, of course, starting with Morgan in 2012. I'd had seven salesgirls, three store managers, and a dozen hair stylists. Donovan had been our art director for eighteen months. Younger Cheekys Chicks worked paid internships, usually during the summer and Christmas season. Dad worked in the printing operation, and his wife helped with shipping. Turns out, Pops didn't mind Idaho. Sure, he hated the snow, but he liked working with Justin, and he loved family dinner with his grandkids, even though his prostate cancer meant he could only eat meat twice a year, on Father's Day and his birthday.

I needed four or five more people, at least. But staffing a company is harder than a store. I remember how excited I was when I convinced Misty, my first back office hire, to work for Cheekys. She was my age; she had been a loyal customer for years; and she was vibrant. That's the best way I can describe her. Misty had a shock of bright red hair and a personality to match. She was a ball of fire.

I hired her to work in the store and provide support for the Facebook page and the website, because in a small company, everybody does multiple jobs. It wasn't long, though, before we ran into a problem: Misty didn't know much about computers, and Cheekys was computer-intensive. If you don't know how to edit, format, and upload files, you can't work on that side of the business. So after numerous false starts and failed learning experiences, I had to let Misty go. That was rough. Firing someone sucks. I lost a great customer and friend that day.

Then there was Angie. I really, really did not want to hire Angie. She had been laid off after thirty years when Conagra shut down their local testing facility, so she was closer to dad's age than mine. She smoked like a chimney, and while we wear comfy clothes at Cheekys, Angie's style was a little too oversize "Raider Nation" sports jersey for my taste.

And Angie was *sloooooow*. I don't mean mentally. She was plenty smart. I mean physically. Angie walked slow. She talked slow. You know the sloths in *Zootopia*? That was Angie. Cute, but not a good partner in a Ping-Pong game. And I'm "Hammy" from *Over the Hedge*. I'm like, "Let's go, hurry up, make a decision, get it done." I just knew Angie was a terrible fit for Cheekys.

Justin insisted I keep an open mind. He met Angie when the fire department put out her major house fire. He got to know her and her husband when he helped them rebuild. He kept telling me, "You need to hire Angie, Jessi. She's a worker. She'll do anything you ask."

Finally, I gave in. I hired her part-time to pack and ship auction items. I hate shipping, as I've said, and that's where you should hire people first: for the tasks you hate.

Angie was amazing. She never made mistakes, no matter how long the neck on that ceramic giraffe, but more important, the customers loved her. The auction is our most interactive group, and Angie always took the time (a *loooong* time) to listen to and help our members. Even at her pace, she got the work done, because she was efficient. And if there was too much to finish, she stayed late or came in on the weekend. She and her husband don't watch television. They don't drink much or go camping. Their weekend hobby is coming into Cheekys with a packed meal and having a picnic while Angie works. They're so perfectly matched. He moves slow, too! And Angie is perfect for Cheekys. Turns out, she's the fastest turtle in the world.

She's my shipping manager now. It takes her forever to hire, but she gets the best people. Shipping used to be my highest turnover area; since Angie took over, it's stable. And it's no drama, except for that one time Justin came running to tell me Angie quit.

"What! Why?"

"I have no idea."

I had fourteen or fifteen employees by then. Everyone was more of a pain in my butt (in loveable ways) than Angie. And I needed Angie. I relied on her. So I ran to the shipping area. Angie had been upset for weeks, it turned out, but she was so calm by nature that even I didn't notice, and I'm a spider in the center of my Cheekys web. I feel every vibration. It took Angie doing something drastic for me to finally sit down and say the most important thing a boss can say to an employee: I appreciated her. There were a hundred ways to get a task done, and I valued her for always sticking with what she thought was best and doing it her way. We worked differently, but that wasn't a problem. In the end, it's what made us stronger together.

They call me the Boss Lady around here. It's my hashtag; it's my email address; it's even the title of this book. I can't remember how or when that started (it probably had something to do with Miranda), but my first nickname was actually the Boss Mare, meaning the lead female horse in a team. But it sounded weird: BossMayor. BossMer. BossMore? So the girls changed it to Boss Molly, since I'm more of a mule anyway, but even here in ranch country some people didn't know what that meant.

Then one day I was down near Boise getting my car washed. There were tons of trucks in the parking lot, but right next to the door was a beautiful convertible. In front, reserving the spot, was a big sparkly sign: Lady Boss.

I was like, "Dang, that is cool. I want *that* one day." I didn't have the nice car. I was driving my Yukalade, and no car wash will ever make that beat-up, scratched-up, two-tone monster look clean. But I figured I could earn the title.

So, yeah, I guess I gave myself the nickname Boss Lady, but my employees made it stick. They use as it as a verbal eye roll: "Sorry, the Boss Lady said we have to do this again." They use it to lighten the mood: "Hey, Boss Lady, what you think of this necklace?" They use it as a term of respect. I still don't have a glittery sign (Christmas gift idea!), but now I'm the Boss Lady on the Hub and our Facebook page, too. It's gotten to the point where if other boutique owners try to call themselves that, girls go, "Umm... you're not the Boss Lady. Jessi's the Boss Lady." (Not something I would say—I want us all to be bosses—but I appreciate it.)

It's more than a fun title. It's useful. I try not to run a selfish company. I want my employees to feel empowered and my customers to feel like part of the family. But being the Boss Lady reminds everyone that Jessi makes the final decision, and my word stands. It's important to have a well-defined chain of command.

It also gives me courage when I doubt myself, which is every day. I'm the Boss Lady. I'm in charge. I have to step up and stand by my choices. That means taking responsibility and admitting when I'm wrong, whether that's to my employees, my customers, or my kids. It means taking responsibility when Cheekys is wrong, even if I wasn't involved. It means going to my employees, privately, and saying, "You were wrong. You messed up. Now how are you going to fix it?"

I haven't used the term "Boss Lady" much in this book, which probably feels strange, given the title. But there's a reason. There were many times in my life I was a Boss Lady. I was a Boss Lady when I walked out on Ben for cheating. I was a Boss Lady when I listened to Hunter and started living for my kids again. I can point to a thousand moments over the years where I was a Boss Lady in my life.

But I didn't *feel* like a Boss Lady until this point—thirty-eight, mother of four, with a million-dollar business and a full staff of employees. I hate the term "Girl Boss," and not just because I'm the exact opposite of the girl who made it famous. I hate it because it's small. It makes us seem childish. Do you know what I felt like when I realized I was a Boss Lady? I felt like an adult.

I know what I'm doing, I thought. *I'm in control. I own my decisions, from the type of dishes in my cabinets to the kind of employer and company I want to be. And because of that, I've earned the right to tell other people what to do, to tell them off . . . and to tell them I love them, even though I need them to do better.*

I earned the right for people to look up to me. That was the hardest thing to grasp, because people were watching Cheekys, and copying what I did, and asking for advice. I hated it. I felt unworthy. Until I finally said, "You know what, I *am* the Boss Lady. I *can* withstand the scrutiny. I can even handle the respect. Because that's what adults do."

That doesn't mean I don't make mistakes. Oh, boy, I make mistakes. This whole book could be called "Jessi's Big Fat Collection of Bad Decisions and Foolish Mistakes." But mistakes are an opportunity to learn and do better, and that's what a Boss Lady does. She stands tall, darlin'. She stands for what she believes in. She shows the world that women can lead.

CHAPTER 17

HEAD MOTHER CLUCKER

When my mentor in the car business, Chris Robin, promoted me to sales manager, he told me, "Your job now, J. D., is to make sure each of your employees has what they need—a new house, a new car, whatever is going to make them happy."

My employees weren't working for me, Chris explained. They were working for themselves and their families. In order to get what I needed from them, they had to see that their hard work paid off in their personal lives.

I built Cheekys on that idea: that as the Boss Lady, the responsibility is mine. I have to give my customers good products. I have to give my retailers good service. I have to make my employees happy, not just on the job, but in their lives, before I can earn a real commitment from them.

That doesn't mean just money, thank goodness, because Cheekys doesn't pay a lot. Around here, starter houses cost $20,000, most jobs are hourly, and eleven dollars per is about as good as it gets for less than ten years' experience. Most of my top employees make more than I do, but I still can't compete on pay with the companies in Boise. I have to offer something more: a fulfilling job that fits their personal hopes and dreams.

I learned that in the car business, too, when I had to confront a salesman, a good family man, who was struggling. He coached a bunch of sports teams; he always talked about his kids. In fact, he spent so much time thinking about them, he couldn't focus on his work.

I told him, "You're not making your numbers. The boss wants me to fire you. But I want to offer you a deal instead. How about this? Every day, as soon as you sell a car, you can leave."

He was skeptical. "What do you mean?"

"Just what I said. If you come in at nine, and you sell a car at nine-thirty, you can go home. You can do that every day, as long as you sell a car first."

He looked at me like I was crazy. He knew he was failing. He had expected to be punished. This sounded like a reward. *It was motivation.* That man immediately started selling twice as many cars, because I gave him what he really wanted: the chance to spend more time with his family.

Treating employees like that isn't softhearted. Far from it. I'll never forget the day Chris Robin called his six sales managers into a meeting and said, "Each of you has to fire someone by the end of the day. You're not making your numbers. That means you're not doing enough to help your employees succeed. So one of them has to go home tonight and explain to his wife and kids that he got laid off, and that's on you. You're the one hurting that family."

I was the only manager who didn't have to do it. I made my numbers. And believe me, that was a far better reward than a bonus check. The day Justin and I had to lay off eight good, hardworking men from his coatings business was one of the worst of my life. Not having to fire someone was my perfect motivation. And Chris Robin knew it.

That kind of individual attention is hard in a growing company. Thirty employees may not seem that large, but that's a lot of people to know and understand. There was a sense in New Plymouth that Cheekys had shriveled up and gone away, but it wasn't true. I may have moved the retail store to Fruitland, but the heart of Cheekys has always been and will always be in New Plymouth. I was there fourteen hours a day, pouring my heart and soul into what we were building. We were bigger and growing faster than ever.

But we no longer catered to local customers. The sign that used to be out front was leaning against the wall in a back hallway. We locked the door on Plymouth Avenue and used two smaller doors around the corner on Maple Street, past the Zion Bank and a one-seat barbershop where Dudly had been cutting men's hair since 1960-who-knows-when. To passersby, Cheekys was no more noticeable than an anthill, tucked away behind metal doors and frosted glass.

But inside...we were a freaking anthill. We had combined three rental properties into a maze of repurposed, barely connected spaces: the old store, the old salon, the old storage area, then an exit to the street and a second door to the decommissioned post office turned shipping center. Nobody had an office. There weren't departments, just desks crammed into open spaces. The old store was stuffed with accessories—bead necklaces in a hundred colors, hats, beer cozies, makeup kits, turquoise jewelry, and bath bombs—while the clothing was folded and organized by size and color on twenty-foot metal racks in the shipping area at the opposite end of the maze. People were scurrying back and forth (like ants) all day long to match jewelry and hats with pullovers and shirts: picking orders, setting up product shoots, mixing and matching for discounted groupings. Everyone shouted questions at each other, not to mention playful insults.

I was the worst offender. My door was always open, because I didn't have a door. My space had been built as a hairstyling station, so it had walls on three sides, but two were half-walls only three feet high. I had a desk you couldn't see, it was so covered in samples; a sofa you couldn't sit on because it was so covered in more samples; and a set of shelves buried in fabric books, color swatches, papers, and coffee cups. I'm not saying you have to be messy if you're busy. I'm just saying that's my excuse.

Since the space was close to the middle (the boss should be in the middle, not the corner), I was constantly yelling into the anthill about emails, the status of orders, or lunch. At the same time, employees were constantly dropping in to ask my opinion. Hey, Boss Lady, is this sample necklace color okay? (No.) Hey, Boss Lady, what should I tell this store in Oklahoma about this item? (The truth, even if it hurts.) How should I enter this data? How should I ship this order? Where's the extra toilet paper? Whatever the job, Justin and I had done it. Over the years, we'd done every task and used every machine, pricing gun, merchandise display, and hand truck at Cheekys.

So 90 percent of the time, my response was, "Think about it. Is this a question you can answer yourself?"

That's rule number one: *Let every employee take ownership of their job, and if they aren't taking ownership, make them.* We developed new shipping software last year, and Brandon, who runs the crew that picks and compiles for Angie to box and ship, was boggled. He came over a hundred times to ask me how to handle something.

I said, "Brandon, that's your system. You better figure out how to use it, because that's what I'm paying you to do."

Brandon was new. He didn't want to risk being wrong. It was my job, as the Boss Lady, to show him that honest errors would be tolerated, and that he was perfectly capable of correcting and eliminating his own mistakes.

I do that with my family, too. When Hunter was stressing over the last project he needed to (barely) graduate high school, I refused to help him. He complained, but I told him, "That degree won't mean much if you don't earn it."

"Thanks for letting me prove myself," he said when he passed. I never thought he'd be that proud of his degree. Honestly, before he transferred, I never thought he'd graduate. *But he took personal responsibility.*

It's not enough to help employees earn it, though. As a Boss

Lady, you need to reward them. *Give everyone a win*, as I say. Let them know they aren't just filling a slot; they have value. A win could be as simple as acknowledging their great ink color choice, their viral Facebook post, or congratulating Brandon— sarcastically but truly, because he prefers it that way—on getting through the day with no mistakes.

In 2016, I hired a second designer. She was intimidated. The manic Cheekys anthill is a lot for new employees, and Donovan could be a perfectionist. After I rejected her first three or four designs, I could tell she was frustrated. So when she came to me with a new design she was proud of, I approved it.

The fact is, I was neutral to the design. I wasn't convinced anyone would like it. But she sure did, and she needed a win.

You know what? She was right. The Chicks loved her shirt, and it sold well. That didn't change our relationship. Putting through a design I wasn't 100 percent about was a one-off. I'm still going to Boss Lady her designs, even if I'm now more confident with and open to her style. But it changed her relationship with the company. She had designed a successful product; that made her a contributor. It made her proud. It motivated her to keep pushing hard so she'd get more successful designs on more successful shirts. Recently, when her first shirt was copied exactly by Wish, she was more angry than I was. She "owned" that design, even if the finished products said Cheekys.

That's a win—for her and for me.

Yes, I do that one at home, too. When the twins neglected their job cleaning the chicken coop, for instance, I decided not

to push them. *Let them take ownership.* After a few weeks, as the
poop piled up, I was regretting that decision. Then, one day, I
came home and they were like, "Mom, mom, come here, we
have something to show you!"

It was a pile of chicken poop, shredded newspaper, and shav-
ings three feet high. It was just sitting in the yard, not where it
was supposed to be, but they were so proud, because they'd done
it on their own. They hadn't even been asked. So...

"I'm cooking steaks for you tonight," I said. "And you know
what? Addy's going to help me while the two of you relax.
Because you earned the right to be taken care of."

It's not about control. It's not about them doing the job exactly
like you wanted. Honestly, I don't care for half the stuff Justin
builds, because it's not exactly what I had in mind. But I learned
a long time ago to bite my tongue and thank him. What's more
important, Justin being happy or me getting exactly what I
imagined?

And a few weeks later, "You know, babe, I hated those plant-
ers, but you were right. They work really well there. Thank you."

It's not easy. My staff called a meeting a few months ago and
sat Justin and me down. They said, "We need you to quit micro-
managing us. Let us do our jobs." I was almost crying, because
I wanted to do that, I thought I was doing that, but I put everything into Cheekys. I built the company with relentless work
out of the wreckage of my life, and it meant everything to me.
Even the paper used to stuff the boxes meant everything to me,
because I kept saying Cheekys was everyone, together, but in

the end, down at the core, it felt like me. And thanks to my employees, I could see the truth: I was scared to let go. I was scared to embrace the "us." Even when I thought I was loosening my grip, I was still holding tight.

"Trust us, Jessi," they said. "That's why we're here."

I listened. I've tried hard to change. Because that's Boss Lady, too: *noticing and acknowledging mistakes.* When my employees are struggling, I talk to them. I'm honest. I ask, "What do you think is going on? Why isn't this working?"

They know there's a problem. Usually they can identify it, even when they're the problem.

"Okay," I say, after I hear their explanation. "What would you do if you were me?"

That's a second chance. That's their opportunity to be a Boss Lady. I still have to fire them sometimes if they can't figure it out, but I've given them support, and I've given them a chance. That's what the meeting was: an honest conversation. It was my employees turning my lessons and beliefs back on me.

Dang, thinking of it that way makes me feel pretty good . . .

Not every issue is the same, of course. Some call for a different approach. I could see Kristie was struggling with the store, for instance, so at our six-month meeting, I pushed the account books aside and addressed the problem head on: "This isn't like you thought it would be, is it?"

"No," she admitted. "It's so much harder."

Running the Cheekys salon was mostly scheduling, since the stylists paid rent and bought their own supplies. Kristie was good at that, and she loved hair. Running a store meant selecting merchandise, controlling inventory, pricing, staffing, and constantly putting yourself out to remind the local community and loyal customers that you were there for them. She was right: It was much harder.

"It's too much," Kristie said. "I'm not happy. I don't think I can do it. Honestly, if I thought I could run away, I would."

I said, "Kristie, you can do this. You are a bright, talented woman, and I'm not going to let you quit. But I will bring in a store manager to help you."

I called Morgan, who had been away from Cheekys for more than a year styling hair in Boise. "We need you," I said, which made her very happy.

"I'm twenty years old," she liked to say, "and I'm running a store."

A few months later, Kristie pulled me aside. "Thank you," she said. "I needed that."

She didn't mean Morgan, although they made a great team. She meant my faith and being held accountable. Kristie's had a hard run. She's been with some bad dudes—cheats and drug addicts and angry men who didn't treat her with respect. It shakes your confidence. But Kristie's a good person. Everybody likes Kristie, even the men who treated her bad. They just hated themselves and took it out on her. When I showed her what we all knew—that she was better than she believed—Kristie overcame her doubt. She rented a house in New Plymouth. She found a great boyfriend. Her nine-year-old son was over last year to swim in my aboveground Bi-Mart pool, and he said: "I'm proud of my mom. She's so cool. She owns a store."

The situation unfolded just the opposite, though, when I

hired a third designer, a younger woman with a funny and sarcastic personality. I realized the first morning she wasn't a good match with Donovan, but I left their relationship alone, hoping they could work it out. Finally, after a few weeks, she said, offhand but meaning it, "Does he always smell like alcohol at ten in the morning?"

That hit me like a brick. I knew Donovan was drinking. You can't hide that in a town with only two bars and one liquor store. I thought I was downplaying it for a friend, but that's not what I was doing. I was ignoring a problem.

It ran deeper than alcohol. Donovan had moved to Boise to live with his girlfriend, and he'd been complaining about the commute. For months, he'd been bugging me to rent him a satellite office in Boise so he could work down there. He'd been complaining about the noise and disorganization of the anthill, the new employees, the boredom of tiny old New Plymouth, where the only place to go was the bars. He was causing the friction with the new designer, not the other way around. He was making her uncomfortable on purpose. *Because Donovan didn't want to be here anymore.*

I love Donovan. Not the way I love Justin, or Ben once upon a time, but the way you love someone you've worked with intensely, and with whom you've done life-changing things. The designs Donovan and I created launched me into manufacturing and launched Cheekys into a brand. I was proud of that, and so was he. We had a special relationship. But we'd outgrown it.

That was scary, but that's what Cheekys was meant to do. I wanted every person who worked for us to grow, become confident, and find their passion. If that meant they dedicated themselves to Cheekys, fantastic. If it meant they left for other opportunities, just as good. Outsiders didn't understand that. They thought someone leaving was a sign of a problem. But I didn't want to hold anyone back because it benefited me. Every employee works for themselves and their family. I have to put their ambitions first.

Donovan was a freelance designer when I hired him. Now he had experience as a full-time art director. He knew what he wanted. He had a home studio where he created far-out hipster (he would kill me for using that word) shirt designs, which Justin printed for him in small batches. He didn't want to draw anatomically correct cows and "Lucky Not Blessed" horseshoes for Cheekys; he wanted to create psychedelic tigers with diamond collars.

But neither Donovan nor I was acknowledging this, so he was acting out, probably hoping for a push into a new life. I was ignoring his behavior, because I didn't want to let a valuable employee go. That was a serious problem. Good workplaces are a balance. Everyone has to work together, encourage each other, and do their part. That started with the Boss Lady. By letting one person get away with bad behavior, especially my highest paid and most beloved employee, I was unbalancing the whole staff.

So I let Donovan go. Well, Justin did. I know my limits.

Donovan was angry. He said some harsh things. But a month later, he admitted that he was relieved. He's a gypsy now, traveling the West in a trailer with his laptop and his cats. He's happier. I'm happier. Cheekys is a better place, now that everyone wants to work here. And Donovan still does freelance work for us whenever I ask.

That experience reinforced an idea I've learned, then forgotten (or conveniently ignored) five or ten times over the course of my career: Sometimes the best thing you can do for a person is let them go.

We're Americans. If anyone asks us about quitting anything, the answer is supposed to be: hell no. Never surrender. Never change course. Make them throw you out, if you must go, kicking and screaming.

Well, guess what? Sometimes the courageous decision is to move on. I was right to quit my marriage to Ben, after all. He wasn't right for me. And the same was true of the second Cheekys store manager I ever hired.

She was a local girl: young, smart, great fashion sense. But her marriage was falling apart, and her life unraveled along with it. Finally, I sat her down and said, "What would you do if you were me?"

She said, "I'd have fired me two months ago."

"Why?"

"Because I'm really messed up right now."

"Well, what do you want me to do?"

She started crying. She said, "I can't lose this job, Jessi. If I do, everyone I've ever known will think I'm a failure."

(continued)

That's a hazard of a small town, especially if you've never left. It can start to feel like the whole world is watching and judging you. But I told her, "That's the wrong reason to stay, and you know it."

We worked out a graceful exit that allowed her to keep her pride. Eventually, she divorced her husband and cleaned up. She's been working at local bars for about five years, and she's happy. She found her place. She's one of my favorite employees that got away.

A few years later, I noticed Miranda was miserable. She had always been the happy kid. Sure of herself, popular but kind, graduated at the top of her high school class with all the ribbons and tassels. This mopey, sad-eyed, snappy girl wasn't Miranda. So I took her aside. "What's going on?" I asked.

"Nothing."

"Don't lie to me. I know you too well."

She hesitated. "I hate college," she said, gushing tears.

The traditional story you hear about small-town kids is that they want to go to college, can't afford it, and wind up trapped. That wasn't Miranda. Her parents had college degrees. They worked for the BLM. Her mother ran a triathlon in Thailand, for goodness sake. Miranda could have done anything she wanted.

"I want to go to cosmetology school," she said. "I know that sounds foolish, but I want to make people look pretty, because when they look good, they feel good about themselves. That's my dream. But I'm afraid my parents will be disappointed in me."

I said, "Girl, you need to go home and talk to your parents tonight."

She did, and they weren't disappointed. They said they loved and supported her, no matter what—especially since she wasn't dropping a quickie marriage or a pregnancy on them. So Miranda quit college, enrolled in cosmetology school, and I don't think I've seen her unhappy since. (But I have seen her married, happily so.)

So walk, if you know what you're doing isn't what you want. Move on. Being a Boss Lady isn't about suffering through the wrong thing. It's not even about being a boss. It's about doing what you want with your life, no matter the risk.

CHAPTER 18

I LEFT MY HEART IN NEW PLYMOUTH

It's complicated in a small town. I didn't rely on New Plymouth to feed my family—thank goodness, we'd have starved long ago—but we were deeply intertwined. I closed my retail store, and the coffee shop went out of business. We sent so many packages through our one-room town post office, the postal service assigned them a second truck. Angie and Brandon probably kept the Pilgrim Market in the red with their cigarette purchases. (Angie even smoked slow!) I finally bought myself a new car, an electric blue Dodge Charger, and people just had to comment. It's such an odd codependence. It's like: Y'all are ignoring my company, and yet you're all up in my business!

It was the same with my employees: We were all up in each other's business. I mean, our printing facility was in my backyard. When we had company get-togethers, they were in my backyard. Justin is a Traeger fanatic, so we invited employees over to grill out all the time, even in the winter. I couldn't have avoided my employees if I wanted to, which I didn't, because I knew them outside the job. Almost everyone I hired was a Cheekys Chick or a long-time customer. Or they came to me through a friend or relative in town, which was complicated. You can get crushed in a small town for firing the wrong person's sister, despite everyone knowing she deserved it.

Even Brandon, the only man in our New Plymouth headquarters—it was twenty hens and one very hen-pecked rooster—was a friend of the company. We call him the Jolly Gay Giant because he's six foot six, always smiling and, you guessed it, gay.

"I've been wearing your earrings and bracelets for years," Brandon told me the night we were introduced by my sister-in-law. I just shook my head and smiled. A year later, I hired him.

Brandon and New Plymouth got along fine, until the teenager behind the counter at Garbonzo's refused to serve him pizza because he was gay. Did Cheekys rally around him? Of course we did. Hunter was so pissed, he started a Facebook and Twitter campaign. But this isn't a story of small-town homophobia. The couple in line behind Brandon walked out when they heard the kid refuse him service, saying they would never eat there again. Within hours, the owner, who hadn't been in the restaurant at the time, called to apologize. If anyone in New Plymouth agreed with what happened, I never heard about it. Sorry, y'all, we aren't as easy to pigeonhole as you think.

That was an easy situation to handle; others are harder. Cheekys' strength is that we're (almost) all small-town women from similar circumstances who care about each other. But the close proximity of a small company, just like a small town, can lead to complications.

I learned that early on when I had a few employees over for a barbeque. One girl's husband got drunk, then angry—some men, when they see their wives having a good time, get threatened by their independence—and said he was taking their two-year-old home. His wife ran after the truck to stop him. When she came back, her face was bloody.

She said she slipped on the ice, but we didn't believe her. Her husband was a self-proclaimed asshole and proud of it. I knew he could be violent, and I knew she was miserable. She had opened up to me about it months before. But now the proverbial shit had hit the fan, because there was blood on my driveway, and one of my guests had called the cops.

I told her she needed to leave him. I told her to live with me until she got her life straightened out, because there was no way a mother should go back to a man like that. She kicked him out instead. Then she started freaking out: about custody, about finances, about what everyone in town was saying. I pushed her to stay strong. To believe in herself. I told her a good woman would do that for her kids. What a cruel thing to say. It wasn't helpful; it just added to her guilt. When she took him back, I admit, I was disappointed in her.

Pretty soon she was blaming me for everything: the police report, the arguments, the troubles in her marriage. She was more miserable than ever, but I'd lost the ability to help her, because I was in the middle of it now, and she saw me as part of the problem. Before long, I lost her as an employee, and then as a friend.

As a boss, you can't impose your solution on an employee's personal situation, no matter how badly you want to. That's true even if the answer seems obvious, *and even if you've been in that situation yourself.* I once dated a man who knocked me to the floor and kicked me until I passed out. I was recently looking at my prayer journal from that time, and it said, "I don't understand why he spits on me and doesn't love me. What's wrong with me?" That's when I remembered: That man spat in my face. Twice. On two separate days.

So I was speaking from experience when I told my friend she shouldn't go back to the man who punched her. But my experience didn't matter, because it was her decision, not mine. I should have offered comfort. I should have told her I would always be there for her, no matter what she decided. When I went past that, I lost a young woman who meant a great deal to me.

Abuse is tough. It's hard to talk about, much less handle. That's why so many ignore it. They pretend it doesn't exist. But I've seen it everywhere I've lived, and at every stage of my life. Domestic and sexual abuse is more common than we want to believe, and it is devastating. It destroys lives. It destroys families. It can destroy companies, too.

It can tear women apart. I saw that with my friend, and I experienced it with my sister, too. Several years after I escaped, my mother left W. Her mom moved to Texas to live with her and help take care of my sisters. Soon after, Grandma married a man she worked with at Walmart. Soon after that, he started sexually abusing my youngest sister. When my middle sister found out, she told him if he stopped, he could do it to her instead. She was about ten, and kids think that way. They don't understand their power. They don't know grown-ups like that are the weakest, most pathetic people on earth. Their "step-granddad" started sexually abusing them both.

After he was arrested, I went to Texas to help. Late one night, the older of the two started telling me what happened. She was eight years younger than me, so she was only three when I left. And she was W's biological daughter, so she'd been treated differently. The closest we'd ever been was probably the night I helped deliver her on a dirty mattress in an abandoned house. I was the first person to hold her, before our mother took her away.

But I held her again that night, for the second time. I told her, "I hear you. It's terrible. I understand."

She jerked back. "You don't understand. How could you understand?"

Her anger shocked me. "I was raped, too," I said.

"Really?! By Alvis?"

"No. Not by him."

"By who?"

I hesitated. I'd taken this conversation in the wrong direction, and I wanted out. So I looked into the next room and saw a bottle of Jack Daniel's black label on the table.

"Jack," I said.

"What's his last name?"

"Black."

"That's a lie," she said. And she left. We never spoke about it again. We've never really spoken since.

I didn't want to hurt her. That's why I wouldn't tell her the truth. But I made a mistake. She was eleven, I was nineteen; we were too young to deal with this situation. So I handled it wrong, and I hurt her. I hurt us. But I didn't want her to know that...that...

My God, I do not want to talk about this. I don't want to say what I have to say here. Because it hurts. Because it rips me in half even now. Because I'm already afraid people will read this book and say, "Jessi's done all right...for a woman."

"Jessi's done all right...for a high school dropout...for a country girl...for someone who just sells clothes and junk and woman stuff."

I don't want people to say, "Well, dang, Jessi's done all right... for a sexual assault victim."

I'm not a victim. I felt like one for a long time, but I can't feel like that anymore. I can't let anyone steal my dreams, and I can't let what they did to me diminish what I've done for myself. I don't want praise with an asterisk. I don't want to be graded on a curve. I want to be called what I am—a businesswoman, *a Boss Lady*, an amazing mom, a faithful partner and wife—and I want to be judged, if you have to judge me, on Cheekys, which I am damn proud of, and which is my heart and soul.

I'm not writing this book alone. I have a writing partner. He's from Georgia, but he comes to New Plymouth and hangs out in my backyard. He told me I wasn't allowed to mention that. He said, "You have to pretend I don't exist. That's how it works."

I said, "That's not going to happen, because the only reason I'm writing this book is to show other women it can be done. They can live their dream. I don't want them to think I run a company, *and* I'm a mom, *and* I had time to sit down and write a whole book, because nobody can do that. There's not enough time in the day. So this isn't a request. I have to tell them I had help."

Now, he's turned my words back on me. He said, "If you're going to be an example to other women, Jessi, you have to be honest. Right? You have to tell them everything."

"But why this?"

"Because it happened. And you're not the only one."

He's right. I know that. I know there's power in speaking out, and there's freedom, too. So as much as I hate to say it:

I was sexually abused by my "stepfather" W, who was my younger sister's biological father, from the age of two to eleven. I was raped and sexually abused repeatedly while he documented, filmed, and photographed it. I can't remember a time before I was sexually abused, because the abuse started before I was old enough to form and keep memories, but I've lost long stretches of my childhood, and I fear my mind has locked them away for my own safety. I know others knew of the abuse, because others were involved. Nobody did anything to stop it, not even my mother, until I finally told my father's new wife what was happening to me. That's when she and Pops refused to send me back, and when—no doubt after being confronted—W let me go.

He never really let me go, though. I always lived in fear of him. I always worried he was going to find me and kill me, like he always said he would. I thought everyone would judge me, and find me dirty or broken, if they knew what he had done.

I remember the day W died. It was 2011, right before we opened Cheekys, and I was on a one-day camping getaway with Justin. There was no cell reception, but when I walked to the showers, for a brief moment, my messages came through, and I saw a two-word text from my baby sister: *He died.*

I panicked. I should have felt relief, even joy, but it wasn't like that. Instead, those two words hit me so hard, I couldn't breathe. I made it to the shower and lost myself crying, but not for him. I hated him. It was a burning hatred. I don't know what I was crying for.

Then I heard the shower room door open, and I screamed. I've always been terrified—so terrified it makes my heart stop to think about it right now—to shower. I will not shower if men I don't know are in my house. It took me a long time, and I mean decades, to feel comfortable showering in hotel rooms. I don't know why that is. I don't *want* to know why that is.

It was only Justin. I don't know why my man thought a campground shower could ever be romantic, God bless him, but he undid me so bad that I never saw him. I never saw anything but black-and-red closing over me, and then I hit the floor. The next thing I remember, I was at the campfire, with Justin bone pale beside me. He looked as terrified as I felt. He was afraid he'd broken me forever.

Two years later, I went to the Dallas Market with a couple friends. On the second day, I woke up and knew what I needed to do. I said, "Can we do something different today? There's a place I need to go."

We drove three hours to the strip mall in Wichita Falls. It had been twenty-five years. I thought it was gonna be different, but it looked exactly like it did in my memories: trash in the parking lot, peeling paint, broken signs saying "XXX," with that hideous collapsed storefront in the corner and that terrible, terrifying fake lighthouse out front by the road. But there was a tall chain-link fence blocking access, and a sign saying the property was up for public auction.

When I saw that sign, I started crying, and I couldn't stop. My friend tried to hold me, then pull me into her arms, but I clung to the fence, barely able to breathe I was crying so hard, and I wouldn't let go. That was the moment I knew he was gone. I was free. I would never have to go back inside. But I wasn't crying just for that. I was crying because I knew no other little girl would ever again have to live through what happened to me. At least not there.

A few years later, I discovered an employee sleeping behind some merchandise in the store-turned-warehouse. She kept breaking down in tears, and each time she did, it bent her over in pain. I knew it was broken ribs, and I knew how she'd gotten them, because these things gather over time.

I wanted to hug her. I wanted to say *I know*, and *I understand*, and *I've been there, too*. I wanted to tell her what to do: *Leave the monster. Believe in yourself. Don't let him take your confidence and steal your soul*. But I knew I couldn't, because I'd gone through this with seven employees already. You can't be the Boss Lady when it comes to their lives. They have to take ownership. They have to come to you.

At the end of the day, she did. She told me what had happened. I told her Cheekys was here for her. That she had hard times ahead, but we would support her—financially and emotionally—no matter what she decided. She went back to her husband, but things didn't turn out well. She started drinking, and then she started sleeping around. I knew she couldn't afford Christmas presents for her kids, so I told her to come to my house that weekend, I'd give her a few hundred dollars to clean up the auction stuff piling up on my porch. She didn't show. She was too hung over.

She ended up pregnant. Shortly after that, we lost her. She left Cheekys, and she's with another man now, and he's no better than the last.

I wish her story wasn't like that. I wish the world wasn't like that. But I've been around long enough to know I can care, but I can't live another woman's life. The best I can do is let her know this company will always support her, *always*, as best we can.

I have a similar situation with another employee now. I know the husband well, and I like him. I don't condemn him. We all have demons. Lord knows I have plenty. But his are visible, and they're hurting him, and more important, they're hurting his wife.

I've barely talked to this employee about her situation. I can never step that far into her life. She's too valuable, as a worker and friend, to risk losing her. But she knows how I feel. She knows I want the best for her. Last Christmas, I gave her a wish book. I wrote many wishes in it, but this is one that meant the most to me:

I wish your husband could see you the way I do.

CHAPTER 19

CORE BITCHES

Eric Arnault, another mentor in the car business, introduced me to the concept of core and fringe employees. Fringe employees are important, he said, but they come and go. This isn't their dream job. Core employees are vital to your business. You have to identify and take care of those people. They will guide your company, and if you train and treat them right, they can run it if needed.

I've simplified that concept into a saying, since sayings are what I do: Behind every successful woman...is a tribe of other successful women who have her back.

Nobody is fringe at Cheekys: not an employee, a wholesale customer, or a woman who buys a single item. I have ten women around the country, all originally customers, who read our emails and Facebook queries. If the question is easy (like sizes, dates, or policies), they answer it. If not, they forward it to us at headquarters. It's a fringe job, I guess, since I've never met most of them, but it's not fringe to me. Those Chicks are vital, because without them, I couldn't meet my goal of responding to every customer within an hour.

But I have an inner circle of women who have earned my trust. I'm going to be very upset if you're reading this book ten years from now and all these women aren't working at Cheekys, because these are my girls. I call them the Core Bitches. And yeah, I'm a Bitch, too, because when the Bitches talk, it's never *I*. It's *us*. Cheekys is *our* company.

There are five of us, but it was almost six. When I was thinking about forming the group, I took the girls to the apparel market in Las Vegas. I wanted to know them better and see how they interacted with one another. Vegas, right? Girls' trip to Sin City!

When I bought my electric blue Dodge Charger in late 2016, I put a little something special on the front: a personalized license plate that says Bad Mom. Yeah, that's a middle finger to those who have belittled and looked down on me because of the custody situation with my kids. Fine. Whatever. I can embrace that now. I love cruising Plymouth Avenue in my bright blue muscle car, windows down, sunglasses on, and a huge coffee from the Jolts & Juice in Fruitland in my hand: *Yo, bitches, I'm still here. And I got six boxloads of scoop-neck tees all up in my trunk!*

I actually got the license plate because I love the movie *Bad Moms*. Bunch of smart, taken-for-granted, hardworking woman cutting loose? That's my jam. I wanted to tear up the Vegas Strip. We were moms. We were badasses. Let's get it on, Bitches!

You know what we actually did? We worked and slept...and talked about our kids.

Like a bunch of moms.

It was clear one woman didn't fit with the group. This wasn't the girl who got drunk and called a fellow Chick fat. In fact, she did nothing wrong. It was a personality thing, and personality matters in your core. I have dinner with my Core Bitches. I travel with them. Most important, I'm vulnerable with them. I tell them my fears and failings, because I want them to know the Boss Lady is human, and they can be human with me, too. When we trust each other like that, nothing can break us.

So the Bitches became five:

Me, whom you've met.

Erika Mata, my wholesale director. Erika's husband is a successful car salesman, and for years she was a receptionist/bookkeeper at the dealership. But she knew she could do more. I tell Gustavo all the time: "You guys let something special get away, because your wife can *sell*."

Erika manages our retail network, and she always makes her numbers, even though growth isn't our priority. We're careful about who sells Cheekys, so Erika interviews and researches each applicant to make sure they fit our values. We never approve a store in a current client's market, because we don't want to hurt their business, and that's complex now that we have almost 4,000 outlets selling our products.

She keeps our clients happy, too. A month before Christmas 2016, southwest Idaho received so much snow, a third of our farmers' onion sheds collapsed. Ten towns lost either their only school or only grocery store when their roofs gave way under twenty feet of snow and ice. There's one road to New Plymouth. The pickup and delivery trucks couldn't get down it for three weeks, so we couldn't ship—right before Christmas! Our customers understood. The delay hurt them in their most important season, but they stuck with us. That's a testament to Erika, but also to those storeowners. Cheekys has the best costumers.

The second Core Bitch is Erica Alfaro, my lead designer. She and Erika Mata are both second generation Mexican American, and they share a name, obviously, so there was a rivalry. But Bitches before Stitches, right? They worked it out.

I wanted to hire Erica for a long time. She had a degree in fashion design, and she brought a beautiful portfolio to her job interview. But she was pregnant. She hated her job in Nampa digitizing embroidery patterns and designing restaurant menus, but it paid more than Cheekys, and it offered health insurance. I don't offer health insurance (few employers here do). I don't even have health insurance myself. So Erica turned me down.

We stayed in touch. I checked in every month or so to see if there was anything her family needed. I never mentioned the job. Okay, maybe a little, but mostly we talked about the baby. Erica was talented. She was wasting that talent in Nampa, and she knew it. I wanted her to remember Cheekys was here.

Finally, after a year, she asked me to lunch. She said, "I hate my job, Jessi. I'm not happy. I don't care if it's less money, I want to work for you."

Less than a month after she started, her husband, Jose, quit his job as a social worker in a disagreement over how the facility was being run. He was hoping to go back to college for his master's, so Justin offered him shifts in the print shop to help with the bills.

Erica loved that. She was crushing on the job, because Cheekys empowered her to create her own designs. Now she and Jose could commute together from Caldwell. I often saw them in my backyard, laughing and having lunch. When Erica got pregnant again, Jose asked if he could come on full-time. We happily agreed. He's our print manager now, working with Justin, Pops, and Hunter—if our headquarters is a Hen Den, our printing facility is definitely a Man Cave. Jose is too educated and talented for printing, but he's happy, because we stumbled on the perfect motivation for him and Erica: the opportunity to work with each other.

Then there's Audrey Austin, my social media manager. She was a Cheekys Chick for four years before I convinced her to run our Internet operation. It's dangerous to hire a friend, as I've noted. Liking someone doesn't mean they'll be a good employee. But Audrey is a *great* employee. She is wonderfully, delightfully OCD. I mean, the girl brings her own sheets and towels to hotels—even the Venetian in Las Vegas. She makes a list of tasks every morning and, unlike every other person in the world, she actually completes it. When Audrey started changing the clothes on the mannequins before photo shoots, I noticed they hung a little better.

"Oh, I steam iron them first," she said.

Dang. Smart!

Audrey's job is technical, so she's more behind the scenes. That doesn't mean she isn't vital. Every company needs a person *who gets all the shit done*, and that's Audrey. We couldn't keep our operation running smoothly without her.

And last, there's Rachal Messersmith. Rachal applied for the social media position, and I liked her. She was smart and personable, she was a mom, she had run a successful MLM (multilevel marketing) business out of her house for years, and she was from a large Mormon family. A lot of Mormons own boutiques. Many, like Rachal, start in MLM networks, which have deep roots in their tight-knit community. I liked the idea of having someone on staff who understood the importance of the Family Meal.

So I hired her to work with Kristie in Fruitland. I love Morgan. She's been with me forever. But Morgan was young, hungry, and looking for a man. I knew she would soon be moving on, and that was for the best. Sometimes, in business and in life, people outgrow each other. I hired Rachal to be Kristie's Suzie.

Two months later, I stole her. I brought her to New Plymouth as my right hand. This was late 2016, and the business was exploding. In March of that year, *Inc.* ran a story about the "former Outback Steakhouse waitress" (I didn't tell them 5 percent of it, y'all) who created a $2.8 million a year retail business in tiny New Plymouth, Idaho. By August, I realized Cheekys was going to top $7 million. That's when I brought Rachal over and formed the Bitches.

Our first big project was the Bitty Boxes: a pre-purchased monthly box of products, selected by our staff. Each box cost forty-five dollars and contained at least three items: a piece of Cheekys clothing, a piece of jewelry, and an item from outside our usual offerings.

The Bitty Boxes were a great way to increase sales, but they had other advantages, too. They introduced new designs. They focused our products, since each month had a theme. And they decreased manufacturing costs, since I knew in advance how many shirts or pieces of jewelry I needed—about 700 for the first box.

Scaling like that was convenient for Cheekys merchandise, but essential for the outside items. I'm a market junkie. I'm constantly finding unusual items I love from small, often one-woman companies. But manufacturing unusual lipsticks or a funky makeup bag was a lot more expensive than a shirt or jewelry, and I was struggling to give these cool women large enough orders for their prices to work in my market. The Bitty Boxes allowed me to buy 700 scented oil kits instead of twenty-five, so everyone's price came down, and I was finally able to introduce the Chicks to my favorite funky finds, while giving a boost to some talented, deserving women.

The other draw of the Bitty Boxes was interaction with the Chicks. Buyers knew the theme of each box, but they didn't know what was inside. So a Bitty Box was like opening a present on Christmas morning. It was as intimate as we could get with our customers, especially the ones who lived hundreds of miles away.

We had been posting videos on our Facebook page for years. That summer, we started streaming on Facebook Live. It was poorly shot (by me), unscripted iPhone footage from inside the anthill, but the Chicks loved it, because it was real. They could see our piles of junk. They could see our lived-in desks and casual outfits. They could see that our rural, goofy, blue-collar image wasn't a lie. It was who we were.

That led us to a very smart decision: a live reveal of the first Bitty Box. We had been advertising the box for months. Now, just as they arrived in people's homes, we would open one on Facebook Live and reveal what was inside.

I chose Rachal for the livestream, because she was funny, chatty, and approachably pretty. She had straight hair with highlights, a youthful face, smart-girl glasses, and braces. Yes, braces. On her teeth. Rachal was thirty, with two children, but she looked seventeen, and somehow she pulled it off. I wasn't jealous at all. No way!

The operation was bare bones. We half cleared the storage corner behind my office and set up a folding table. Rachal and I talked a little about what she should say, but there was no script. We weren't even sure how long the live feed would last. At the scheduled hour, I just started filming with my iPhone and Rachal started talking.

The Chicks *loved* it. I had a computer set up so I could watch the feed on Facebook, and after thirty seconds the screen started filling with comments. *Love this. So fun. Love her. I want that top. Can I buy it if I didn't get the box?* We had sold 700 Bitty Boxes, which was a lot of work. We formed a seven-person assembly line to fill the boxes, and it still took a week. But almost 25,000 people watched the reveal.

I looked at Rachal and I was like, *Dang, girl. Guess you're our spokesperson now.*

We started scheduling Facebook Live videos at least twice a week, for promotions and new items and holidays and birthdays and anything we could think of. We spruced up the "set" by clearing the boxes, adding a high wooden table, and hanging a cow skull we found in a back room on the wall. Beyond that, we just got less professional.

Rachal and I weren't just live-streamers. I was teaching her to run the company with me. So we'd be ordering merchandise, picking jewelry designs from samples, or managing clients, and suddenly Audrey would yell, "It's four fifty-eight. You're on in two minutes!"

Crap. Forgot to watch the time. Again.

So we'd scramble to get it together, often running into place seconds before the scheduled time. When Rachal couldn't find her notes, I filmed live while she looked for them. Once, while scrolling the comments, I accidently switched to selfie mode. Suddenly, our feed was nothing but a close-up of the top half of my face. Both Rachal and I busted out laughing, because... what a klutz!

I started talking to Rachal from behind the camera. I'd say, "Hey, you forgot that item," or, "I don't think that price is right. Erika"—screaming to Mata off-screen—"what's the price on that new scoop-neck with the cactus?"

At first, I read Rachal the comments from the Chicks so she could respond. Then I started responding myself. I made fun of Rachal when she screwed up, which was all the time. During one feed, Rachal and I got into an argument over whether a drawing on another company's product was a donkey or a llama. The disagreement went on for several minutes, with Chicks sending in their opinions, until we finally compromised and called it a "lladonka." We still talk about the lladonka. We even made a lladonka shirt, and then a lladonka-themed Bitty Box, one of our most popular.

#LladonkaLivesMatter

I'm sure someone stumbling onto the feed from outside our bubble would find it the worst, most amateur thing they'd ever seen. Lladonka? Whatever. You're not clever, you're just a couple regular women having a good time in a messy little room.

Sure enough: "This is so stupid," someone posted one day. Didn't bother me, but boy, did it bother the Chicks. Suddenly the screen filled with women saying she was the stupid one, please go away, and other less polite things. The Chicks are very protective of us.

At one point, they became obsessed with Rachal's braces. They started a hashtag, #ShowRachalsTeeth. Every time Rachal was on: #ShowRachalsTeeth.

Then someone started the even more popular #ShowJessisFace. They heard my voice all the time, but I was never on camera— except for my forehead, that time I hit selfie mode. I played along, pretending I was about to step into the frame, but I was never going to do it. I hated the way I looked, with my sweaty hair-bun, old Cheekys tee, and forty-year-old-mom bloat. After everything, I still didn't have the confidence to show the world who I was.

Then one month, we had a weak Bitty Box. That happens. Everything can't be your best. This was the month I tried to use an American manufacturer for my shirts, and they messed up the order. So we had to scramble for an alternative, and I wasn't happy with the way the box came out.

I didn't feel right sending Rachal out for the reveal. I didn't want her to be stuck out there alone when the Chicks started complaining. So I decided to join her on camera. If Chicks were going to be mad at somebody, I wanted it to be me.

By then, we were selling 1,500 Bitty boxes a month, and Chicks had started waiting to open their boxes until the moment Rachal opened hers. So we were live-streaming our reveal, while dozens of Chicks were live-streaming their reveals back to us. I was on camera, laughing and joking, but I was also keeping an eye on the computer, dreading the moment their excitement at #SawJessisFace turned into disappointment.

It never happened. I was being too hard on myself, like I always am. The Chicks loved the box. And they loved me on camera. They didn't think I was fat. They didn't think I was frumpy. They started text-chanting: *Jessi's face! Jessi's face!* And to my surprise, I was comfortable with that. I'm on camera almost every day now, and I love it. I hop on without a second thought, whenever I'm needed. That's the power of friends. When good people support you, you can do anything.

(That's not a universal feeling around here. Some employees *hate* being on camera. I'm looking at you, Erickas. #ShowErickasFace.)

I didn't understand the power of the Chicks, though, until Rachal's sister in Arizona disappeared. Her husband claimed they had a fight and she stormed out, saying she was never coming back. That didn't make sense. Rachal's sister had five children. The oldest was autistic. She never left that girl alone, not for a minute.

Rachal was a wreck. When her sister didn't turn up the next morning, she was sure something was wrong. I hugged her, and her whole body was shaking. I said, "Let's ask the Chicks for help."

We blasted out the message: *Rachal's sister is missing. Here's her name. Here's her description. Here's where she lives.*

We started getting messages back immediately.

I live in Arizona. I have a friend in Arizona. My mother-in-law lives in Arizona. We are spreading the news. We are going out to look for her right now. Don't worry, Rachal. We are going to find her.

Messages poured in from around the world: women telling Rachal they loved her, they were praying for her sister, everything was going to be all right.

It wasn't. The police found her body two days later, buried in pinecones and pine needles in the forest across from her apartment building. She had been shot with a pistol in the mouth, but that wasn't what killed her. It was probably to obscure her identity. The coroner said she had been beaten to death, then thrown off the balcony of her third-floor apartment. Her husband had broken almost every bone in her body.

She was the second sister Rachal lost to domestic violence. In high school, her oldest sister died of a gunshot to the abdomen. The police ruled it a suicide, but Rachal's family never believed it. Three years later, her fiancé came to their home and confessed to accidentally killing her during an argument. That night, he killed himself.

We found out about the tragic ending in Arizona less than half an hour before Rachal was scheduled to go live with that month's Bitty Box. I knew she was crushed. I could see it. Why wouldn't she be? She'd lost a sister. Five children lost their mom.

"You don't have to…"

"I can do it," she said.

"No, Rachal. Let me."

"The Chicks have been so good to me. They need to know what happened."

"I'll tell them."

"No, Jessi," she said firmly. "I need to do this."

I have never watched the livestream. I lived it. That was enough. I lived through those terrible first minutes when Rachal was crying. I was crying. We were all crying. There must have been hundreds, if not thousands, of Chicks crying, too.

Then Rachal did something extraordinary: She pulled herself together, and she smiled. This was the first time Rachal had been live without her braces, a big deal in Cheekys World. We had given her a card: "Congrats on becoming an adult." We had blasted the news to the Chicks: *This is the one! #ShowRachalsTeeth.* But her smile, on that day, was so much more than a meme. It was a message. It said: They can't beat us, because we're strong. We're going on, despite the heartbreak. And we're going to win, because we have each other.

Well, y'all, I hate to say it, but Rachal and I parted ways about a year after all this took place. I'd tell you how I feel, but I honestly can't say. I've had a hundred different feelings about it, and that's only in the last week. That's what happens when you lose someone you care about.

What I *can* tell you is this: Don't lie to yourself. Trust your intuition. I knew what was coming six months before it happened, but I didn't act. I had employees trying to draw my attention to certain things, but I didn't want to look. Members of my Core Bitches came and talked to me privately. That's a hard step. It can feel like a betrayal. But when I didn't pay enough attention, I turned the betrayal back on them. I gave my best employees a reason to doubt me.

I tell myself I did it out of love. I wanted it to work out with Rachal, because I cared so much about her. And that's true.

But it was mostly fear. I put Rachal out as the face of the company because she was young and pretty, and I wasn't. She was my filter. With her beside me, no one would see too

(continued)

clearly who I was. That was my big mistake, because it wasn't fair to her. And it wasn't fair to me, either.

The day we parted didn't scare me. It was the next day, when I had to go live on Facebook and tell the Chicks she was gone. I thought they might hate me. I thought, *Maybe they've only been coming for her.* But it wasn't like that. The Chicks didn't hate me. They understood. They were encouraging. They didn't look down on me for my extra chins and my flat hair. My need for a "pretty filter" had all been in my mind.

Nothing is indispensable. That's an important thing I've learned over the years. Not me. Not her. Not that product or that idea. It's the company and the community—it's all of us, together—that matter.

But I'm the Boss Lady, so I have to set the tone. I have to define what Cheekys is and what we stand for. I can't be afraid of being judged. I have to be confident in myself and show my true face to the world.

That goes for everything in life. You can't change for the neighbors. You can't try to be like the moms on TV. You can't forget your values because a company offers a large contract or an extra dollar per hour. That's a betrayal. It will bite you in the end.

But here's the thing: You're good, girl.

No, you're great.

So listen to your allies. Notice red flags. Value your intuition. And above all, believe in yourself. That's what will make *you* happy, and everyone who depends on you.

CHAPTER 20

THE NUMBERS GAME

I'm a numbers girl at heart. I have a white wipe-off board visible to every employee that tracks our daily, monthly, and yearly sales by category: store, Internet, and wholesale. The Core Bitches meet to discuss them every week. Justin and I discuss our shipping and printing figures every day. I sat with Kristie (Morgan moved with a boyfriend to South Dakota) every month. I asked her: "How were sales this month? Which items sold best? Which categories are lagging, and which are growing?"

She gave me her opinion. Then we looked at the numbers. Guess what? Perception isn't reality. Sales of new items get noticed, but it's the classics—the pieces you overlook because they've been steady so long—that make a business profitable.

It's the same with customers: New ones are awesome; welcome to the club! It's fun to watch your followers click up to 500,000, then 600,000 and beyond. But it's the core Chicks who matter: the people and stores that always order and have been with us through the rain. I don't want any of those Chicks, whether Dusty Darlin's (Western girls) or Boho Babes (urban gypsies) to feel overlooked.

My main project now is making our community less dependent on Facebook. The algorithm changes too frequently, and their constant tinkering is a danger to every small business on the platform. Every year, they crush some of my friends, like a stupid kid crushing ants. And it's not just Facebook. I know a boutique owner whose Instagram account was seized and destroyed without warning. She lost more than 100,000 contacts, the backbone of her business, because she accidently infringed on the copyright of some company called Popsocket.

Even PayPal accidently almost put me out of business. I was at $7 million a year in sales, but I still couldn't get a traditional bank loan, so I was reliant on their credit program. Then, *at their suggestion*, I switched to Braintree Payments, another division of the company. Suddenly, my credit line dropped from $85,000 to $5,000.

I called them. "The algorithm thinks you're a new customer. You have to build your credit back."

Fine. I wish you'd told me that before I switched, but fine. I went out and sold $150,000 through their system in four days. My credit line didn't budge.

"The algorithm says you shouldn't be able to sell that much. It thinks you're having a going out of business sale."

"Look, I've been on PayPal for years. You can see my track record."

"It doesn't matter. The algorithm is our god. It won't increase your credit line for at least three months."

Okay, she didn't say the algorithm was their god, but it was implied. And their algorithm is a cruel, arbitrary, and ignorant asshole.

That's why you have to own and secure your own data. You have to interact directly with your customers. You have to be as self-sufficient as possible. Social media is a great place to start, because it's cheap. Cheekys wouldn't be where we are today without Facebook. But to be a Boss Lady, you have to move beyond it. The more you cut out the technological middleman, the more stable your business will be.

That's why, in 2017, I started developing my own app and ordering system. After a few months, I invited the six hundred Chicks in a private buying group to beta test it for me. One of our social media taggers in North Carolina suggested that. How's that for being vital to the business?

We spent months working through the kinks with our betas, so when we finally took down our website and launched the new interface in October 2017...the software company somehow forgot to include a "continue shopping" button.

The Chicks were squawking. Our sales dropped. But we fixed it, we got the interface back online, and...the Chicks hated it.

I mean, they *haaa-ted* it.

Instead of fighting them, I put the old site back in place. The Christmas season was approaching, and I was focused on having a strong December. I set a goal: our first million-dollar month.

No, I wanted to hit a million and half between Thanksgiving and Christmas, which would push us past $10 million for the year. Now that sounded special. That nice round number created a nice, clean "Story of Success." If we did $10 million in a year, nobody could say Cheekys was just a tiny woman's store in a nothing town anymore.

So I threw the whole company into our Black Friday sale. It was weeks of new merchandise, inventory, promotions, sales calls, livestreams. I was up at four a.m. Idaho time, working on the Facebook page and answering questions. When my twenty-year-old cousin, Abby, who was staying with us for Thanksgiving, left at six-thirty a.m. with Addy and Sterling to go Black Friday shopping in Boise, I was in my pajamas. When my uncle got a call from her at nine a.m., I was *still* in my pajamas, pounding away on my keyboard. I only stopped working when I saw the look on his face.

"There's been an accident," he said.

I figured it was a fender bender. The Yukalade was a beast. Then Sterling called me. He couldn't talk. He was so upset, he was having trouble forming words. A man, who turned out to be a witness, got on the phone: "We're at mile marker twenty-two," he said. "The ambulance is on the way."

I was up and dressed in a shot. Justin was in Ontario at the Home Depot. He left his full cart in the aisle and sprinted to his truck. We made it to mile marker twenty-two at the same time, even though on a normal day he was a half an hour farther away.

I couldn't believe the scene. Abby had come up too fast behind a slow car, swerved to avoid it, and gone off the road. The Yuka-lade skidded down an embankment, flipped end over end three times, and came to rest in an alfalfa field. The front end was crushed. Glass was everywhere. The interior was covered with blood. Justin had a chain saw in the back (because, of course). The force of the crash was so powerful it flew out of its case, through the shattered windshield, and embedded up to the hilt in the ground.

Thank God the kids were wearing their seat belts. Thank God. Abby had severe whiplash, but was otherwise unhurt.

A shattered window cut up Sterling's hand and lower arm. He had a laceration on his head, but he wasn't in danger.

Addy was being loaded into an ambulance, covered in blood. When I climbed in with her, she vomited blood everywhere. They almost had to remove me, I was so shaken, but she needed me—my daughter needed me—so I rode with her to Nampa.

Her injuries weren't as bad as they looked, thank God. She had shattered her nose, which caused most of the bleeding and vomiting. They stitched and bandaged her, then kept her for observation. She was so sore she could barely move, but we took her home that night.

After she fell asleep, Justin and I hugged each other and cried. Cheekys had had the biggest sales day in our history. We sold three times as much on Black Friday 2017 as we'd sold on any day before. I couldn't have cared less. I hadn't thought about Cheekys for one second since the accident.

Addy didn't stay quiet long. She woke up screaming and couldn't go back to sleep. She was jumpy and anxious the next morning, and so was Sterling. Addy cried on and off all weekend. She had a huge bandage on her nose and two very black eyes.

I called the Bitches. "You guys are running Cheekys," I said. "My children need me."

Then a Cheekys Chick called to ask if Addy liked horses. She owned a therapy riding center, and she offered to take Addy out as many times as she needed. There is nothing in the world quite like a horse to soothe an anxious child. I laughed with joy when I saw Addy on Cuervo, finally smiling.

Lucy Hegge from Rietdyk's called the first day, and she kept calling. She kept saying, "Come to Portland. Relax. Get away. Stay with us." I said no at first, but after a few weeks, it was clear Sterling and Addy were still affected by the crash.

So we loaded the Suburban (RIP, Yukalade, you were a beautiful beast). Hunter stayed home with his friend Kolby, who was basically living with us while he finished his last year of high school, but the rest of the family made the long drive to Portland together. I knew it would be uncomfortable for Sterling and Addy on the highway, so we took it slow and made numerous stops. We stayed on Don and Lucy's boat, which the kids loved, but otherwise I can't remember any of the places we visited.

I just remember constantly looking over my shoulder, checking to make sure the kids were okay. Cheekys was falling short of my $10 million goal. We didn't even make our first million-dollar month. But who cares? Sterling was in his baseball cap, with the brim pulled low. Jack had on his Western button-up. Addy was wearing the fuzzy white jacket Justin's parents had given her because her old jacket was covered in blood. They were pushing and joking, like children, but I could see the love they had for one another in Sterling's huge smile, Jack's sly looks, Addy's comfort, now that she was with her brothers, despite her swollen nose and blackened eyes.

This is Boss Lady, y'all. *This is happiness.* This is what the dream looks like for me and millions like me. And it's here for you. It's not impossible. Anyone can achieve it. It takes hard work. It takes smart work. It takes love, and staying true to your values, and never giving in, but this is an American family, so anything is possible.

Even in Idaho.

BACK TO NEW PLYMOUTH

"So, um, Jessi, why do you love New Plymouth?" That was my editor's big question after reading a draft of this book.

It surprised me. I thought: *Isn't it obvious?* Because it's beautiful. Because I don't have to worry about crime or fight traffic. Because you have to drive three hours from New York City for a weekend away, but I'm already here. I can see mountains from my backyard. When I sit with Justin in our camp chairs late on a summer night, and we stop talking, just for a moment, it's quiet. The sky is full of stars. Our big white dog, Neva, lopes out of the field. She lies at our feet. And I'm happy, because this is the most peaceful place on earth, and it's ours.

"But what about the people? They don't seem very supportive."

Yeah, they're people, and people are the same no matter where you go. Some are mean. Some are suspicious. Some don't care enough about their neighbors to try to understand what they do, which is human nature, after all. A few care too much. But most are wonderful people. Friendly people. Giving people.

I have hundreds of supporters in New Plymouth. I have incredible friends. It's a great community, and it's an honor to live here. The only person I really have a problem with is the principal who treated Hunter so poorly, and I'm not the only one. He was promoted to school superintendent, a position high enough for more people to realize he was a bully. The town tried to get rid of him, but for months he refused to go. It was such a big scandal, it made the news in Boise.

During that period, one of the popular moms called about my experience with the school. At the end of the conversation, she paused, and then she said, "I know you feel your family got run out of town, Jessi. I am truly sorry about that."

Maybe that seems like a small thing to you. Maybe it was a small thing. But it meant a great deal to me.

They say that, in the country, if your parents' parents didn't run the store, you're an outsider. I guess that's true, to a point. I felt like an outsider in New Plymouth for a long time. But it's not the whole truth. To succeed, here or anywhere, you need roots like an oak and the spirit of a gypsy. You have to dig into your piece of earth and draw strength from its past, even as you embrace the freedom of the future. But you don't have to inherit your roots. You can grow them.

That's what Justin and I are doing in New Plymouth. We're digging deep. We recently bought three unused buildings on Plymouth Avenue, including the original Cheekys location. We'll fix up and rent two of them. Hunter has been managing our printing operation for the last year; he's talking about maybe opening a print shop for the public. It might be nice. He'd get a chance to run his own business and prove himself to the people of this town. That's a win for him.

It would be a win for me. I think it would be a win for New Plymouth, too.

But the biggest win for me right now was reorganizing Cheekys retail. I love Kristie, but the store had stagnated while the rest of the business grew, and it was time to close the shop in Fruitland. No licenses from now on. No more pieces of Cheekys not under my direct control. I don't know what Kristie has in her future, and right now, neither does she. That's okay. Her purpose wasn't running a Cheekys, and two years of struggle made that clear. Without that burden, she can discover who she was meant to be. And I will be here for her on that journey, always, because she's a Chick.

For me, though, closing the Fruitland store wasn't a retreat. It was a homecoming. The two-year moratorium is up, so we're clearing the merchandise from our old storefront and turning it back into the showplace New Plymouth Cheekys store I always wanted. Donovan designed a gorgeous new sign that looks like a 1950s movie marquee; the silo dressing rooms and barnlike counter are being restored; Justin is preparing to tear down our last barn for more weather-beaten wood. We'll have a coffee bar instead of a salon, so we'll probably run late with the rebuild, and we'll have to call in every friend of Cheekys within twenty miles—and Texas, since my ex-husband, Ben, will no doubt help us again. We'll work ourselves sick and have more fun than any group of people should have trying as hard as we do.

"It's stressful working here," Mandy, the Mother Hen whose

daughter was kicked by a horse, told me, "but it's the best kind of stress." I can't imagine that's ever going to change.

After we build it, will they come? There are plenty of Cheekys fans in New Plymouth, but can I convince the rest of the town we're more than a "little corner junk shop"? Can we make New Plymouth a destination for our 50,000 loyal Chicks, even though we're on a back road? Can we bring people from all over the Payette Valley—or Idaho—or even the world—to this gorgeous, struggling, frustrating, perfect little town? Can we make New Plymouth as vibrant as it was before the highway six miles away separated us from the wider world in 1957?

I'm eager to find out, because I'm an entrepreneur. I live for new challenges. But it doesn't matter. Not really. My heart is here. My roots are deep in New Plymouth, even if they aren't old. But my business is worldwide. If I never make another dollar in New Plymouth, my family will be fine, and so will my employees. But I want to help this town grow and prosper, especially by embracing its past: the old Western architecture, locally owned shops, and the stronger community that will form when farmers and ranchers know they don't have to go to the Hammer Truckstop or the Walmart in Ontario, they can get what they need on Plymouth Avenue.

It won't be easy. Nothing is. We'll always be under the microscope here. We'll always have someone unhappy with something we've done or said. But that's just part of being in a tight-knit community, especially a rural one. Embrace the challenge. Enjoy it. *Own it, girl.* Maybe when Addy's daughter takes over Cheekys in 2053, we'll be accepted here. Maybe we'll even be considered a pillar of the community. A Boss Lady can dream, can't she?

Until then, when people ask me why I love New Plymouth, I'll think of the smiles on my kids' faces when they ride their foot scooters along Plymouth Avenue. I'll think of the last three waterwheels and the smell of freshly cut mint. I'll think of the summer concert I organized at the rodeo grounds in 2016, as a fund-raiser for our volunteer fire department. I grew up with corral dances. Some of my only happy childhood memories are dancing barefoot to country music in barns. We work very hard out here, especially the ranchers and farmers. Most of us don't get a vacation. A lot of ranchers don't even get weekends. I wanted to give everyone a night to remember.

I got lucky: I hired Ned LeDoux. You know him, right? Son of Chris LeDoux, the Hall of Fame rodeo champion and number one best-selling country singer who sold more than 3 million albums before his untimely death in 2005…

Okay, I know some of you don't know him. But guess what? Millions of us do, because that's our culture. That's what we celebrate at Cheekys: cattle, country music, and cold beer on a hot summer night. Nobody has ever embodied that, in my mind, as perfectly as Ned LeDoux. He didn't haggle over price. He showed up at the Boise airport alone with nothing but a duffel bag and a guitar. When I asked if he wanted anything, he said, "Just a six-pack of original Coors Light and a comfortable bed, that's all I need."

Then he hit the stage, and Ned LeDoux put on a show. He played his songs, but he played his father's hits, too. It didn't bother him that his father's songs were the ones that made the women grab their ranchers and hit the dirt. I wish you could have seen it: a beautiful August sky, the mountains, the Idaho cowboys with their wide hats and wider handlebar mustaches, dancing with their wives to Ned LeDoux, who had nothing but a beat-up acoustic guitar and a bunch of songs made famous by his dad. The whole town was out, from kids to retirees, and Addy was there, too, dancing with Grandpa Roberts like there was nothing better in the world, and nothing else that mattered after all.

We're oaks. Our roots are deep, and we won't be moved.

And we're gypsies. Our jewelry and apparel travel the country. Our message travels the world. Maybe a few people will even read this book. But in the end, everything comes back to this little spot of earth, with its horseshoe streets and its rodeo grounds, its two-block downtown and its pride. Cheekys is from New Plymouth, Idaho, population 1,538, for better and for worse, and so am I.

And I wouldn't want it any other way.

ACKNOWLEDGMENTS

I guess this is the page where I thank and acknowledge all the people who helped make this book possible, but I know if I named names my list would be forever long and I would surely forget one of the most important people—someone like my dad or little sister. Clearly I could never have made it this far in life without God, these amazing kids, my husband Justin, my friends, my co-workers, my mentors, my sisters-in-business, and even all the hurtful folks who made me into who I am. I definitely needed all the publishing people, like my book agents Brandi Bowles at UTA and Peter McGuigan at Foundry, my co-writer Bret Witter, my editor Beth de Guzman, and all the managing editors, assistants, artists, publicists, marketing gurus, and salespeople I haven't even met yet but who found value in this book. I want to thank each person who has read this far and taken these tools to heart—the men and women who hustle and do something good every day...either for themselves or, even better, for someone else. I want to acknowledge every person kind enough to recommend this book to a friend or colleague in the belief that it will make a difference. And I especially want to thank with all my heart the Chicks and Core Bitches: You inspire me and drive me every day to be better than I was yesterday, you love me despite my flaws, and you share this community. It's not one; it's all. Always.

xoxo,
The Boss Lady

AUTHOR'S NOTE

Everyone suffers sometimes. Not every relationship goes as we would like. But abuse—whether verbal, psychological, emotional, or physical—is never acceptable, and being the victim of abuse is nothing to be ashamed of. It's hard to speak out. There has been violence and emotional abuse in my life that, even in my own book, I couldn't share. So don't feel your chance has passed if you haven't spoken out. You don't have to hide. You don't have lie, to yourself or to others. If you are in an abusive relationship, talk to someone who loves you: a parent, a grandparent, a sibling, a friend. Tell them what is going on, and ask for their help. If you don't have someone you feel comfortable confiding in, call a professional, such as the National Domestic Violence Hotline: 1-800-799-SAFE (7233). I've been where you are. Friends of mine have been where you are. You're not alone.

ABOUT THE AUTHORS

JESSI ROBERTS was raised in west Texas and started working full-time to support herself at sixteen. In the early 2000s, she was recruited to Boise, Idaho, to work in sales and management at car dealerships. In 2003, she was one of Idaho's youngest ever recipients of the most accomplished individuals under forty citation—and she didn't even have a high school diploma. In 2011, after four children, a two-year return to Texas, and a failed business venture, she and her husband, Justin, founded Cheekys in the tiny farming town of New Plymouth, Idaho (population 1,538).

The first year, their small store made $43,000—*gross*, not net. But they kept building. First, through Internet sales; then through manufacturing; and finally by designing and selling their own line of clothing, jewelry, and accessories for rural and small-town women. By 2017, Cheekys was making nearly $10 million a year, mostly through Internet sales and a network of more than 4,000 small boutiques that sell their merchandise.

Cheekys now has thirty employees, mostly women, and three buildings in New Plymouth, including a soon-to-be-completed expanded and remodeled "showplace" Cheekys store in New Plymouth's two-block downtown strip. Cheekys' reach is international—its loyal fans, known as Cheekys Chicks and numbering more than 500,000, live around the world—but the heart and soul of the company will always be in rural Idaho, where Jessi and Justin live with their four children in a farmhouse on four acres two miles outside New Plymouth.

BRET WITTER has co-authored eight *New York Times* bestsellers, including the number one best-sellers *Dewey* and *The Monuments Men*. His books have sold more than 3 million copies worldwide and been translated into more than twenty languages. He lives in Decatur, Georgia, with his wife and two children.